The Flavors of
BON APPÉTIT
2007

Seared Wild Salmon with New Potatoes and Dijon Broth
(page 80)

The Flavors of
BON APPÉTIT
2007

from the Editors of Bon Appétit

Condé Nast Books

New York

For *Bon Appétit* Magazine

Barbara Fairchild, *Editor-in-Chief*
Tricia Callas O'Donnell, *Contributing Editor, Books*
Marcy MacDonald, *Editorial Operations Director*
Carri Marks Oosterbaan, *Editorial Production Director*
Michelle Alderson, *Editorial Production Manager*
Zoë Adnopoz, *Editorial Administrator*
Marcia Hartmann Lewis, *Editorial Support*
Susan Champlin, *Text*
Shayna Sobol, *Copy Editor*
Karen Hallal, *Research*
Elizabeth A. Matlin, *Index*

For Condé Nast Books

Lisa Faith Phillips, *Vice President and General Manager*
Tom Downing, *Direct Marketing Director*
Deborah Williams, *Operations Director*
Lyn Barris Hastings, *Associate Marketing Director*
Eric Killer, *Marketing Manager*
Angela Donadic, *Marketing Associate*

Design: Monica Elias and Ph.D

Front Jacket: Milk Chocolate-Peanut Butter Sandwich Cookies (page 228)
Facing Page: Top: Carrot and Caraway Soup (page 25)
Middle: Braised Lamb Shanks with Coriander, Fennel, and Star Anise (page 52)
Bottom: Banana Layer Cake with Caramel Cream and Pecans (page 190)

Published by Condé Nast Books, Random House Direct, Inc., New York, New York.
A wholly owned subsidiary of Random House, Inc.

Printed in the United States of America

Library of Congress Cataloging-in-Publication Data is available upon request.

10 9 8 7 6 5 4 3 2 1

FIRST EDITION

Condé Nast Web Address: bonappetit.com
Bon Appétit Books Web Address: bonappetitbooks.com

Contents

Introduction

Fifty years. The landscape of modern life has changed a bit in that time. We've seen the arrival of space travel and the interstate highway system, CDs and DVDs, laptops and cell phones, food processors and microwave ovens. And a slender bimonthly publication called *Bon Appétit* that debuted in the fall of 1956 evolved into the most popular food and entertaining magazine in the country. In its first half-century, *Bon Appétit* has created a revolution in how we cook, shop, entertain, and—most of all—eat.

The recipes gathered in this book represent the best of *Bon Appétit*'s 50th anniversary year. They also represent the best of what has come to be defined as the *Bon Appétit* style: classic recipes with a contemporary twist. And these recipes promise what *Bon Appétit* is justly famous for: delicious food that you can't wait to eat.

Seared Duck Breasts with Red-Wine Sauce and Candied Kumquats (page 78)

Throughout the magazine's history, *Bon Appétit* has been at the forefront of changing tastes and culinary trends. The '50s cocktail party found a perfect companion in *Bon Appétit,* which has always had a way with fun, inventive cocktails and fantastic finger foods to go with them. That tradition continues into the 21st century: Is there a more contemporary combo than Garam Masala Deviled Eggs (page 12) and Cucumber Gimlets (page 37)? We think not.

When French cooking was all the rage in the 1960s, *Bon Appétit* made that sometimes complicated cuisine understandable and accessible. Over time, as we've moved away from heavy sauces and excess cream and butter, the magazine's recipes have retained the best aspects of French cooking—intense flavor, elegant presentation—in lighter, healthier, and less time-consuming preparations. The Seared Duck Breasts with Red-Wine Sauce and Candied Kumquats (page 78) would be right at home at any one of those French-inspired dinner parties—just as it is on today's dinner table.

In the 1970s, a restaurant revolution pioneered the concept of California cuisine, and *Bon Appétit* introduced millions of home cooks to this fresh approach: cooking with the seasons and with locally grown organic produce. That philosophy has been central to *Bon Appétit*'s recipes ever since, and the Fresh Corn Sauté with Tomatoes, Squash, and Fried Okra (page 131) and the Spring Greens with Orange-Fennel Vinaigrette (page 153) are direct descendants of those first California-style dishes.

The 1980s were all about high-style entertaining, and *Bon Appétit* created perfect menus that featured plenty of tips to help relieve the host's stress and put the *party* back in dinner party. The magazine's do-aheads, ingenious shortcuts, and patented test-kitchen tips continue to make it possible to entertain with delicious style even in today's over-scheduled world. Cauliflower Soup with Seared Scallops, Lemon Oil, and Caviar (page 28) and Caramelized-Banana Tartlets with Bittersweet Chocolate-Port Sauce (page 170) have enough glamour to satisfy an '80s-era millionaire junk-bond trader—and the "do-ability" to appeal to today's busy home cook.

Throughout the decades, America's culinary repertoire has opened up to the world, incorporating all kinds of ethnic ingredients and influences. As usual, *Bon Appétit* was and is on the scene, traveling to exotic destinations and bringing home luscious flavors in recipes that are easy to prepare and fantastic to eat. Perhaps no ethnic trend captivated us as completely as that of Mediterranean cooking, which really took hold in the 1990s. While Italian cuisine has long been popular among the magazine's readers, the Med trend expanded the borders to include all the countries and islands of the Mediterranean, with their emphasis on fresh seafood, olive oil, grains, and vegetables. You'll find plenty of these recipes in this book, such as Linguine Avgolemono with Artichoke Hearts and Green Beans (page 117) or Whole Branzino Roasted in Salt (page 87).

Today we truly are citizens of the world—in a culinary sense, at least. American cooking uses everything from lemongrass to *burrata* cheese, *sambal oelek* to *guanabana* juice. (Yes, there are recipes in this book using all of those ingredients; brownie points—or a Jamaican Coffee Brownie with Pecans [page 230]—to readers who find them all.)

As it celebrates *Bon Appétit*'s 50th anniversary year, this book also showcases everything that has made *Bon Appétit* the best-loved food magazine of the past half-century: beloved recipes enlivened with exotic new ingredients, the familiar and the fantastic, side by side. Where else would

Caramelized Banana Tartlets with
Bittersweet Chocolate-Port Sauce (page 170)

you find Bourbon-Glazed Baby Back Ribs (page 64) and an Iceberg Wedge with Warm Bacon and Blue Cheese Dressing (page 142) next to Char-Grilled Beef Tenderloin with Three-Herb Chimichurri Sauce (page 44) and Quinoa with Moroccan Winter Squash and Carrot Stew (page 106)?

Only in *Bon Appétit*—and only in *The Flavors of Bon Appétit 2007.*

Happy anniversary.

Chilled Watercress Soup with
Green Onion Cream (page 27)

Starters

Appetizers

Soups

Beverages

Shrimp with Artichoke Pesto

1 lemon, halved
2 large artichokes
1 cup (packed) fresh basil leaves
1 garlic clove
1 cup extra-virgin olive oil
1 tablespoon freshly grated Pecorino Romano cheese
1 tablespoon freshly grated Parmesan cheese
32 cooked jumbo shrimp, peeled, deveined

Add juice from lemon half to large bowl of cold water. Cut off artichoke stems; rub cut surfaces with other lemon half. Peel off all leaves. Using spoon with serrated edge, scrape out fibrous chokes from centers. Rub artichoke hearts all over with lemon. Cut into quarters. Chop hearts, basil, and garlic in processor. Add oil and blend until smooth. Transfer to bowl. Mix in cheeses. Season pesto with salt and pepper. Serve with shrimp.

8 SERVINGS

Spicy Lime and Herbed Tofu in Lettuce Cups

DRESSING

- ¼ cup thinly sliced peeled fresh ginger
- ¼ cup thinly sliced fresh lemongrass, cut from bottom 4 inches of 4 stalks with tough leaves removed
- ¼ cup fresh lime juice
- 2 tablespoons fish sauce (such as nam pla or nuoc nam)*
- 2 tablespoons water
- 3 tablespoons sweet chili sauce*

TOFU

- ½ cup diced seeded peeled cucumber
- ¼ cup chopped green onions
- ¼ cup diced seeded plum tomato
- 2 tablespoons chopped seeded jalapeño chile
- 1 tablespoon finely chopped fresh cilantro
- 1 tablespoon finely chopped fresh mint
- 1 tablespoon finely chopped fresh basil (preferably Vietnamese or Thai)
- 1 14- to 16-ounce package firm tofu, drained, cut into ½-inch cubes, patted dry
- 6 large or 12 medium butter lettuce leaves

FOR DRESSING: Puree first 5 ingredients in blender. Let mixture stand at least 15 minutes and up to 1 hour. Strain mixture into small bowl, pressing on solids to release any liquid; discard solids. Stir in sweet chili sauce. (*Can be made 1 day ahead. Cover and refrigerate.*)

FOR TOFU: Combine first 7 ingredients in large bowl. Add tofu and dressing to bowl; toss to coat.

Arrange 1 or 2 lettuce leaves on each of 6 plates. Divide tofu mixture among lettuce leaves and serve.

Available in the Asian foods section of most supermarkets and at Asian markets.

6 SERVINGS

Foie Gras with Bing Cherries and Mâche

12 very thin slices rustic country-style bread (such as pain rustique)
2 tablespoons (¼ stick) butter, melted

¼ cup plus 1 tablespoon cherry balsamic vinegar or regular balsamic vinegar

4 cups (packed) mâche (about 2 ounces)
12 fresh Bing cherries, pitted, quartered
1 tablespoon minced shallot
1 tablespoon grapeseed oil
1 6.5-ounce package chilled block of foie gras (fattened duck liver), cut crosswise into ¼-inch-thick slices

Preheat oven to 375°F. Arrange bread in single layer on rimmed baking sheet; brush lightly with melted butter. Bake until golden brown, about 14 minutes.

Boil ¼ cup vinegar in small saucepan until reduced to 2 tablespoons, about 2 minutes. *(Toasts and vinegar reduction can be made 6 hours ahead. Let stand at room temperature.)*

Combine mâche and quartered cherries in medium bowl. Whisk shallot, grapeseed oil, and remaining 1 tablespoon vinegar in small bowl; add to salad and toss to coat. Season with salt and pepper. Mound salad in center of 6 plates. Arrange foie gras on plates. Drizzle with vinegar reduction. Serve salads with toasts.

6 SERVINGS

Garam Masala Deviled Eggs

6 hard-boiled eggs
3½ tablespoons mayonnaise
3 tablespoons minced green onion
1 tablespoon minced seeded jalapeño chile
1½ teaspoons minced mango chutney
½ teaspoon (scant) garam masala*

Finely chopped radishes

Shell eggs, then cut in half lengthwise. Transfer yolks to small bowl and mash with fork. Mix in mayonnaise. Stir in next 4 ingredients. Season with salt and pepper.

Spoon yolk mixture into whites. Top generously with chopped radishes. *(Can be made 4 hours ahead. Cover loosely and refrigerate.)*

*An Indian spice mixture available in the spice section of many supermarkets and at Indian markets.

MAKES 12

Crispy Yukon Gold Potato Pancakes with Caviar

  1 pound Yukon Gold potatoes, peeled
  1 large egg
  2 tablespoons all purpose flour
  1 teaspoon fresh lemon juice
  ½ teaspoon salt
  ¼ teaspoon ground black pepper

     Vegetable oil (for frying)

  ¼ cup crème fraîche*
  ¼ cup finely chopped red onion
  2 ounces American sturgeon caviar

Using largest holes on box grater, shred potatoes into large bowl. Mix in egg and next 4 ingredients. Transfer potato mixture to strainer set over same bowl.

Add enough oil to heavy medium skillet to reach depth of ¼ inch. Heat oil over medium-high heat. Working in batches, drop batter by rounded tablespoonfuls into hot oil, flattening with back of spoon to form 2- to 3-inch-diameter ¼-inch-thick pancakes. Fry until golden brown, about 4 minutes per side. Transfer pancakes to paper towels to drain.

Top pancakes with crème fraîche, red onion, and caviar; serve.

Available at some supermarkets and at specialty foods stores.

MAKES ABOUT 16

Ginger-Garlic Hummus

 1 garlic clove, peeled
 1 1-inch-long piece peeled fresh ginger
 2 cups garbanzo beans (chickpeas; from two 15-ounce cans), drained,
      3 tablespoons liquid reserved
¼ cup cashew butter
 3 tablespoons unseasoned rice vinegar
1½ teaspoons soy sauce
½ teaspoon chili-garlic sauce*
½ teaspoon freshly ground star anise
¼ cup chopped fresh cilantro
 1 green onion, chopped
 2 whole star anise (optional)

   Crudités

Using on/off turns, mince garlic and ginger in processor. Add beans, reserved bean liquid, cashew butter, rice vinegar, soy sauce, chili-garlic sauce, and ground star anise. Process mixture to coarse puree. Add cilantro and green onion; process to combine. Transfer to bowl; garnish with whole star anise, if desired. Serve with crudités.

*Sold in the Asian foods section of many supermarkets and at Asian markets.

MAKES ABOUT 2½ CUPS

Celebration Dinner for 6

Crispy Yukon Gold Potato Pancakes with Caviar
(opposite; pictured opposite)

Seared Duck Breasts with Red-Wine Sauce and Candied Kumquats
(page 78)

Celery Root Puree

Mixed Green Salad with Sherry Vinaigrette

Pinot Noir

Caramelized-Banana Tartlets with Bittersweet Chocolate-Port Sauce
(page 170)

Espresso

Pizzette with Fontina, Tomato, Basil, and Prosciutto

1 13.8-ounce package refrigerated pizza dough
¾ cup grated Fontina cheese (about 2 ounces)
8 cherry tomatoes (about 3 ounces), quartered
2 tablespoons grated Parmesan cheese

2 teaspoons extra-virgin olive oil
⅓ cup thinly sliced fresh basil
1½ ounces thinly sliced prosciutto, coarsely torn into strips

Preheat oven to 475°F. Lightly sprinkle rimmed baking sheet with flour. Roll out pizza dough ¼ inch thick on lightly floured surface. Using 2¼-inch-diameter cookie cutter, cut 16 dough rounds (reserve any remaining dough for another use). Arrange rounds on prepared baking sheet. Sprinkle rounds with Fontina cheese, dividing equally. Place 2 tomato quarters on each round, pressing gently into dough. Sprinkle tomatoes with Parmesan cheese. (*Can be prepared 2 hours ahead. Cover and chill.*)

Bake pizzette until golden brown, about 12 minutes. Drizzle pizzette with olive oil, then top with basil and sprinkle lightly with salt and pepper. Drape prosciutto strips over. Arrange on platter and serve immediately.

MAKES 16

Lox on Baguette Rounds with Lemon Crème Fraîche

¼ cup crème fraîche
½ teaspoon finely grated lemon peel
12 ounces thinly sliced lox (smoked salmon)
12 ⅓-inch-thick baguette rounds
2 tablespoons chopped fresh chives

Mix crème fraîche and grated lemon peel in small bowl. Divide lox among baguette rounds. Top each with dollop of lemon crème fraîche and sprinkle with chopped fresh chives.

MAKES 12

Cocktail Party for 10

Shrimp with Artichoke Pesto
(double recipe; page 10)

Pizzette with Fontina, Tomato, Basil, and Prosciutto
(at left; pictured opposite)

Lamb Kebabs with Pomegranate-Cumin Glaze
(page 18)

Tuna and Fava Crostini
(double recipe; page 19)

Cheese, Herb, and Sun-Dried Tomato Phyllo Rolls
(page 20)

Caramelized-Onion Dip with Pita Toasts
(double recipe; page 21)

Assorted Cheeses

Baguette Slices

Chardonnay* and *Cabernet Sauvignon

Spirits* and *Mixers

Black and White Chocolate Chunk Cookies
(page 232)

Chocolate Truffles

Lamb Kebabs with Pomegranate-Cumin Glaze

  1 teaspoon cumin seeds
 ¼ cup pomegranate molasses*
 ½ cup extra-virgin olive oil
  3 garlic cloves, pressed
  1 teaspoon dried oregano
  1 teaspoon salt
 ½ teaspoon ground black pepper
 ½ teaspoon ground cinnamon
  1 pound trimmed boneless leg of lamb, cut into twenty-four ¾-inch cubes

  1 large red bell pepper, cut into twenty-four ¾-inch squares
24 small metal skewers or bamboo skewers, soaked in water 30 minutes, drained

Heat small skillet over medium heat. Add cumin and stir until aromatic and lightly toasted, about 2 minutes. Grind cumin in mortar or spice mill. Mix pomegranate molasses, olive oil, garlic, oregano, salt, pepper, cinnamon, and cumin in 1-gallon resealable plastic bag. Add lamb; chill at least 1 hour and up to 4 hours.

Remove lamb from marinade. Thread 1 lamb piece and 1 red pepper piece on each skewer; place on baking sheet. *(Can be made up to 2 hours ahead.)* Cover and refrigerate.

Prepare barbecue (medium-high heat) or preheat broiler. Sprinkle kebabs with salt and pepper. Cook, turning often, about 4 minutes for medium-rare.

Available at some supermarkets and at Middle Eastern markets.

MAKES 24

Fresh Figs with Goat Cheese and Peppered Honey

 ¼ cup honey
 ½ teaspoon freshly ground black pepper
12 fresh figs
 ¼ cup soft fresh goat cheese

Combine honey and pepper in small pitcher; stir to blend. Starting at stem end, cut each fig into quarters, stopping ¼ inch from bottom to leave base intact. Gently press figs open. Spoon 1 teaspoon cheese into center of each. Arrange figs on platter; drizzle with peppered honey.

4 TO 6 SERVINGS

Tuna and Fava Crostini

18 thin baguette slices

4 tablespoons extra-virgin olive oil, divided

8 ounces fresh fava bean pods

1 6- to 7-ounce can solid light tuna in olive oil

¼ cup minced red onion

2 tablespoons chopped fresh Italian parsley plus 18 leaves for garnish

4 teaspoons fresh lemon juice

Favas lend a fresh note here. For the most robust flavor, use tuna packed in olive oil rather than water.

Preheat oven to 350°F. Arrange baguette slices in single layer on baking sheet; brush slices with 3 tablespoons oil. Bake until bread is crisp and golden, about 15 minutes. Set aside.

Bring medium saucepan of water to boil. Shell fava beans, then drop beans into boiling water and cook 1 minute. Drain. Slip beans out of skins. Place beans in small bowl; add remaining 1 tablespoon oil and toss to coat.

Combine tuna with its oil, minced red onion, chopped parsley, and lemon juice in small bowl. Using fork, mash tuna mixture to coarse paste. Season mixture to taste with salt and pepper. (*Baguette slices, fava beans, and tuna mixture can be prepared 4 hours ahead. Let baguette slices stand at room temperature. Cover and refrigerate fava beans and tuna mixture separately.*)

Divide tuna mixture among baguette slices. Top with fava beans and garnish each with 1 parsley leaf.

6 SERVINGS

Beer-Battered Squash Blossoms

1 cup all purpose flour
1½ teaspoons salt
¾ teaspoon garlic powder
½ teaspoon baking powder
1 cup beer

Peanut oil or canola oil (for frying)
24 squash blossoms

Combine first 4 ingredients in medium bowl. Whisk in beer. Cover; chill batter 1 hour. *(Can be made 1 day ahead. Keep chilled; rewhisk before using.)*

Pour enough oil into large saucepan to reach depth of 1¼ inches. Attach deep-fry thermometer to side of pan; heat oil to 375°F. Working in batches, hold stem of each blossom. Lower into batter to coat all but ¼ inch. Fry until golden, about 1 minute per side. Transfer to paper towels to drain. Arrange on platter.

MAKES 24

Cheese, Herb, and Sun-Dried Tomato Phyllo Rolls

1 large egg
¾ cup (packed) grated aged kefalotyri cheese or Pecorino Romano (3 ounces)
¾ cup (packed) grated kasseri cheese or Parmesan cheese (3 ounces)
¼ cup (packed) finely crumbled feta cheese (3 ounces)
2 tablespoons finely chopped drained oil-packed sun-dried tomatoes
2 teaspoons fresh thyme leaves
1 teaspoon chopped fresh marjoram
¼ teaspoon ground white or black pepper

8 sheets phyllo pastry (about 12x14 inches), thawed if frozen
Extra-virgin olive oil

Whisk egg in medium bowl until frothy. Mix in all cheeses, tomatoes, thyme, marjoram, and pepper. Cover and chill until ready to use, up to 1 day.

Stack phyllo sheets. Using sharp knife or shears, cut sheets in half lengthwise, making sixteen 5- to 6-inch-wide pastry strips. Place 1 strip on work surface (keep remaining strips covered with plastic wrap and damp towel to prevent drying). Brush entire strip with oil. Place 1 heaping tablespoon cheese filling in center of strip, 1 inch in from 1 short pastry edge. Shape filling into 3-inch-long log, parallel to short edge. Fold short edge, then sides of pastry, over filling. Continue to roll up, enclosing filling completely. Brush all over with oil; place on rimmed baking sheet. Repeat with remaining phyllo strips and filling. *(Can be made 1 day ahead. Cover and refrigerate.)*

Preheat oven to 350°F. Bake rolls uncovered until filling is heated through and pastry is golden, about 18 minutes. Transfer to platter.

MAKES 16

Caramelized-Onion Dip with Pita Toasts

- 2 tablespoons vegetable oil
- 3 cups chopped sweet onions (such as Vidalia or Maui; about 2 medium)
- 1½ teaspoons garam masala
- 1 8-ounce container crème fraîche or sour cream (1 cup)

  Toasted pita wedges

Heat oil in heavy large skillet over medium heat. Add onions and sauté until slightly softened, about 5 minutes. Reduce heat to medium-low and cook until onions are deep brown and begin to crisp slightly, stirring often, about 40 minutes. Add garam masala; stir 1 minute. Transfer to small bowl and cool completely. Mix in crème fraîche. Season to taste with salt and pepper. Cover and refrigerate at least 2 hours. *(Can be made 2 days ahead. Keep refrigerated.)* Serve with toasted pita wedges.

8 SERVINGS

Corn Soup with Potatoes and Smoked Ham

¼ cup lard
1½ cups diced smoked ham steak (about 8 ounces)
1 cup chopped white onion
½ cup chopped red bell pepper
½ cup chopped green bell pepper
2 garlic cloves, chopped
2 cups fresh corn kernels (cut from about 4 ears of corn) or 2 cups frozen corn kernels
1 10-ounce smoked ham hock
1 medium Yukon Gold potato, peeled, cut into 1-inch pieces
5 cups water

Melt lard in heavy large pot over high heat. Add ham steak, onion, both bell peppers, and garlic; sauté until vegetables are tender, about 10 minutes. Add corn and stir 5 minutes. Add ham hock and potato, then 5 cups water; bring to boil. Reduce heat to medium-low; simmer partially covered 1 hour. Remove ham hock. Season soup to taste with salt and pepper. *(Can be prepared 1 day ahead. Cool slightly. Chill uncovered until cold, then cover and keep chilled. Rewarm over medium heat before serving.)*

8 SERVINGS

Asparagus Soup with Lemon Crème Fraîche

¼ cup (½ stick) butter
1 cup sliced shallots (about 6 large)
2 pounds asparagus, trimmed, cut into 2-inch lengths
2 teaspoons ground coriander
2 14-ounce cans vegetable broth

¼ cup crème fraîche or sour cream
½ teaspoon fresh lemon juice
¼ teaspoon finely grated lemon peel

Melt butter in heavy large saucepan over medium heat. Add shallots; sauté until soft, about 5 minutes. Add asparagus and coriander; stir 1 minute. Add vegetable broth; simmer until asparagus is tender, about 5 minutes. Cool slightly. Working in batches, puree soup in blender. Strain into same saucepan, pressing on solids to release liquid. Season soup with salt and pepper. Keep warm.

Stir crème fraîche, lemon juice, and lemon peel in small bowl. Divide soup among bowls. Top with dollop of lemon crème fraîche and serve.

6 SERVINGS

Creamy Bean Soup with Fresh Herbs and Spinach

3 tablespoons extra-virgin olive oil
3 cups chopped onions
3 garlic cloves, minced
1 tablespoon chopped fresh rosemary
5 cups low-salt chicken broth
2 15- to 16-ounce cans white beans, drained
2 15- to 16-ounce cans garbanzo beans (chickpeas), drained

1 6-ounce bag fresh baby spinach
1 tablespoon chopped fresh sage
Grated Parmesan cheese

Heat oil in large pot over medium-high heat. Add onions and garlic; sauté 15 minutes. Add rosemary; stir 1 minute. Add broth and all beans. Bring soup to boil. Reduce heat to medium-low; simmer 10 minutes.

Working in batches, transfer to blender. Puree until smooth; return to pot. Mix in spinach and sage; stir 1 minute. Season with salt and pepper. Ladle into bowls; sprinkle with cheese.

8 SERVINGS

Avocado Soup with Ancho Cream

SOUP
2½ cups vegetable broth, divided
2 large ripe avocados (about 1½ pounds), halved, pitted, peeled
2 tablespoons fresh lime juice
¼ teaspoon cayenne pepper
¼ cup whipping cream

ANCHO CREAM
1 large dried ancho chile
¼ cup whipping cream

FOR SOUP: Combine 1 cup vegetable broth and next 3 ingredients in processor; blend until smooth. Add remaining 1½ cups broth and blend. Transfer to large bowl. Stir in cream. Cover and refrigerate at least 1 hour and up to 1 day. Season to taste with salt and pepper.

FOR CREAM: Stem chile, halve, and remove seeds. Heat small skillet over medium heat. Add chile; toast on each side until pliable, 2 minutes. Transfer to small bowl; add hot water just to cover. Soak until soft, about 30 minutes. Drain; puree chile in mini processor. Strain into small bowl, pressing on solids. Place cream in another bowl; whisk in 1 tablespoon puree. Chill until ready to use, up to 1 day ahead. Ladle soup into 6 bowls. Drizzle cream over.

6 SERVINGS

Carrot and Caraway Soup

1 tablespoon butter
1 onion, chopped
12 ounces carrots, peeled, sliced
1 teaspoon caraway seeds, crushed in mortar with pestle
1 14-ounce can (or more) low-salt chicken broth

2 tablespoons aquavit*
Chopped fresh parsley

A beautiful bright orange, this soup has the sweetness of carrots and the aromatic nuttiness of caraway.

Melt butter in heavy medium saucepan over medium heat. Add onion and sauté 1 minute. Add carrots and sauté until onion is tender, about 8 minutes. Add caraway and cook 30 seconds. Add 1 can broth. Cover and simmer until carrots are tender, about 35 minutes.

Transfer soup to processor; puree. Season to taste with salt and pepper. (*Can be made 1 day ahead. Cover and refrigerate.*)

Return soup to saucepan and bring to simmer, thinning with more broth if too thick. Mix in aquavit. Ladle soup into bowls. Garnish with parsley and serve.

A Scandinavian caraway-seed-flavored liqueur; available at some liquor stores and specialty foods stores.

2 SERVINGS

Porcini Broth with Wild Mushroom Ravioli

- 3 cups water
- 2 ounces dried porcini mushrooms (about 3 cups)
  Cheesecloth

- 2 tablespoons olive oil
- 2 large shallots, minced (about ¾ cup)
- 4½ cups low-salt chicken broth
- ½ cup dry white wine
- 3 tablespoons dry Sherry
- 1½ teaspoons coarse kosher salt
- ½ teaspoon ground black pepper

- 8 ounces purchased fresh or frozen wild mushroom ravioli
- ¾ cup thinly sliced green onion tops

Bring 3 cups water to boil in medium saucepan. Add porcini. Remove from heat; let soak until mushrooms are soft, about 20 minutes. Place strainer over medium bowl; line strainer with cheesecloth. Strain mushroom soaking liquid (reserve mushrooms for another use).

Heat oil in large saucepan over medium heat. Add shallots; reduce heat to medium-low and sauté until shallots are soft, about 5 minutes. Add mushroom soaking liquid, then chicken broth, wine, Sherry, salt, and pepper; bring to boil. Reduce heat, cover, and simmer 5 minutes. *(Can be made 1 day ahead. Cover and refrigerate.)* Bring to simmer before using.

Cook ravioli in large saucepan of boiling salted water until just tender but still firm to bite. Drain. Add ravioli to hot broth; ladle into bowls. Sprinkle with green onion tops.

6 SERVINGS

Chilled Watercress Soup with Green Onion Cream

SOUP

- 3 tablespoons olive oil
- 2 medium onions, thinly sliced
- 1 large leek (white and pale green parts only), thinly sliced
- 4 cups vegetable broth
- 1 large bunch or 2 medium bunches watercress, thick stems removed (about 4 cups)
- 1 cup half and half

GREEN ONION CREAM

- ¼ cup crème fraîche
- 2 green onions, thinly sliced; dark green parts reserved for garnish
- 1 tablespoon fresh lemon juice
- 2 teaspoons grated lemon peel
- ¼ teaspoon Worcestershire sauce

The flavor intensity of watercress can vary, so the amount needed for this soup will vary, too, depending on whether you like a strong or mild watercress taste.

FOR SOUP: Heat oil in heavy large saucepan over medium heat. Add onions and sauté until soft, stirring often, about 10 minutes. Add leek and sauté 5 minutes. Add vegetable broth and bring to boil. Reduce heat to low, cover, and simmer 10 minutes. Allow broth mixture to cool uncovered 15 minutes.

Place 3 cups watercress in blender. Pour half of warm broth mixture over watercress and blend until smooth. Add half and half and blend until combined.

Transfer soup to bowl. Puree remaining broth mixture in blender until smooth; stir into soup in bowl. If stronger watercress flavor is desired, puree ½ cup watercress with 2 cups soup in same blender. Repeat with more watercress, if desired. Season soup to taste with salt and pepper. Cover and chill until cold, at least 4 hours. (*Can be made 1 day ahead. Keep refrigerated.*)

FOR GREEN ONION CREAM: Mix crème fraîche, white and pale green parts of green onions, and all remaining ingredients in small bowl. (*Can be made 1 day ahead. Cover and chill.*)

Divide soup among 6 shallow bowls. Spoon on green onion cream; sprinkle with sliced dark green onion tops.

6 SERVINGS

Cauliflower Soup with Seared Scallops, Lemon Oil, and Caviar

- 3 tablespoons vegetable oil, divided
- 1 cup chopped white onion
- 1 garlic clove, sliced
- 3¾ cups ½- to ¾-inch pieces cauliflower (from 1 large head)
- 1½ cups low-salt chicken broth
- 1½ cups whipping cream
-   Coarse kosher salt
-   Freshly ground white pepper

- 1 leek (white and pale green parts only), cut into ⅛-inch-thick rounds
- 6 sea scallops, patted dry
- 1 30-gm jar American white sturgeon caviar (about 1 ounce)
- 6 teaspoons purchased lemon-infused grapeseed oil
-   Finely chopped fresh chives

Heat 2 tablespoons oil in heavy large saucepan over medium heat. Add onion and garlic. Sauté until onion is soft, about 5 minutes. Add cauliflower, broth, and cream. Bring soup to boil. Reduce heat to low, partially cover, and simmer gently until cauliflower is tender, about 18 minutes. Puree soup in small batches in blender until smooth. Return to same saucepan. Season soup with kosher salt and white pepper. (*Can be prepared 1 day ahead. Cool slightly. Cover and refrigerate. Rewarm before serving.*)

Blanch leek in small saucepan of boiling salted water 1 minute; drain. Place some of leek in center of each bowl. Heat remaining 1 tablespoon oil in medium skillet over high heat. Sprinkle scallops with salt and pepper. Sear until brown and just opaque in center, about 1½ minutes per side. Place 1 scallop on leek in each bowl; top scallop with caviar. Ladle soup around scallop, drizzle with 1 teaspoon lemon oil, and sprinkle with chives.

6 SERVINGS

Roasted Red Pepper Soup with Orange Cream

    1   tablespoon olive oil
   ²⁄₃   cup sliced shallots (about 4)
    1   15-ounce jar roasted red peppers packed in water
    1   teaspoon sugar
    2   cups (or more) low-salt chicken broth
   ½   cup orange juice

    2   tablespoons whipping cream
   ¾   teaspoon grated orange peel
        Thinly sliced fresh basil leaves

Heat oil in heavy medium saucepan over medium-high heat. Add shallots and sauté 5 minutes. Add red peppers with their liquid. Stir in sugar; sauté 2 minutes. Add 2 cups broth and simmer 5 minutes. Cool soup slightly. Working in batches, puree soup in blender. Return soup to pan. Bring to simmer; stir in orange juice. Thin soup with additional broth, if desired. Season with salt and pepper.

Whisk whipping cream and orange peel in small bowl until slightly thickened. Season with salt and pepper. Ladle soup into bowls. Drizzle orange cream over. Sprinkle with basil and serve.

4 SERVINGS

Dinner with the Neighbors for 4

Roasted Red Pepper Soup with Orange Cream
(at left; pictured at left)

Herb-Basted Chicken with Pearl Barley, Bacon, and Root Vegetable Pilaf
(page 68)

Romaine with Red Wine Vinaigrette

Chardonnay

Chocolate-Cinnamon Gelato with Toffee Bits
(page 217)

Coffee

Caribbean Limeade

   10 cups water
   3½ cups sugar
    6 large bananas, diced
    3 cups fresh lime juice
       Ice
       Lime slices
       Banana slices

Combine 4 cups water and sugar in heavy large saucepan over medium-high heat. Bring to boil, stirring until sugar dissolves. Remove from heat. Mix in bananas. Cover and steep 15 minutes. Strain banana syrup into large pitcher. Add remaining 6 cups water and lime juice. Chill until cold. Fill glasses with ice. Pour limeade into glasses and garnish with lime and banana slices.

12 SERVINGS

Fresh Strawberry Lemonade

   18 cups water
    8 lemons, rinsed, halved
    2 cups (or more) sugar
    6 tablespoons honey

    5 cups sliced hulled strawberries plus whole strawberries for garnish

       Ice cubes

Bring 18 cups water, lemons, 2 cups sugar, and honey just to boil in large nonreactive pot over medium-high heat, stirring until sugar dissolves. Reduce heat and simmer 10 minutes. Remove from heat, cover, and steep 30 minutes. Uncover and cool until just lukewarm, about 2 hours.

Squeeze juice from lemon halves into lemonade; discard peels. Mix in more sugar by ¼ cupfuls, if desired. Add sliced strawberries. Chill until cold, at least 6 hours. (*Can be made 2 days ahead. Cover and keep chilled.*)

Fill glasses with ice cubes. Ladle in lemonade; garnish with whole berries.

MAKES ABOUT 6 QUARTS

Coconut, Strawberry, and Banana Smoothie

¾ cup whole milk
¾ cup canned sweetened cream of coconut (such as Coco López)
1 15- to 16-ounce bag frozen unsweetened strawberries
1 medium banana, peeled, diced

Place all ingredients in blender. Cover; blend until smooth, stopping to scrape down sides. Divide smoothie among 4 glasses.

4 SERVINGS

Spiced Cherry Cider with Kirsch Cream

4 cups cherry cider or cherry juice
2 cinnamon sticks, broken in half
15 whole cloves
2 tablespoons sugar, divided

⅓ cup chilled whipping cream
5 teaspoons kirsch (clear cherry brandy)
1 2-ounce piece semisweet chocolate (optional)

Bring cherry cider, cinnamon sticks, whole cloves, and 1 tablespoon sugar to boil in heavy large saucepan. Reduce heat and simmer until spiced cider is reduced to 2½ cups, about 10 minutes. Strain cider.

Whisk whipping cream, kirsch, and remaining 1 tablespoon sugar in medium bowl to very soft peaks. Ladle cider into glass mugs and top with kirsch cream. Garnish each serving with some grated chocolate, if desired.

4 SERVINGS

White Sangria with Peaches and Frozen Grapes

  2 750-ml bottles dry white wine (such as white Rioja)
  4 cups purchased fresh orange juice
1½ cups Cointreau or other orange liqueur
  2 large ripe peaches, rinsed, halved, pitted, cut into thin slices
  2 lemons, rinsed, cut into very thin rounds, seeded
  4 cups seedless green grapes, frozen
  2 11- to 12-ounce cans chilled grapefruit soda

Combine wine, orange juice, Cointreau, peach slices, and lemon rounds in large jar. Refrigerate until cold, at least 2 hours. (*Can be made 1 day ahead; keep refrigerated.*) Before serving, mix in grapes and soda. Ladle sangria into cups and serve cold.

MAKES ABOUT 16 CUPS

White sangria is much lighter than the red version. Here, frozen grapes take the place of ice cubes.

Lavender Iced Tea

 17 cups water, divided
  2 cups sugar
  2 tablespoons dried lavender blossoms*

 12 tea bags

    Ice cubes
    Dried lavender sprigs (optional)

Bring 5 cups water, 2 cups sugar, and lavender to boil in large saucepan, stirring until sugar dissolves. Boil until reduced to 4 cups, about 14 minutes.

Bring remaining 12 cups water to boil in large pot. Remove from heat. Add tea bags; steep 5 minutes. Strain into very large pitcher. (*Syrup and tea can be made 1 day ahead. Chill separately until cold. Cover; keep chilled.*)

Fill glasses with ice cubes. Pour 1 cup tea into each glass. Stir in 4 to 6 tablespoons syrup, adjusting to taste. Garnish with lavender, if desired, and serve.

*Also called culinary lavender buds; available at natural foods stores, at farmers' markets, and by mail order.

MAKES 4 QUARTS

Jamaican Rum-Ginger Zinger

      2 cups water
      2 ounces fresh ginger, unpeeled, finely grated
      1 teaspoon plus ¾ cup fresh lime juice
      1 tablespoon (packed) golden brown sugar

    1½ cups dark rum
     ¾ cup Simple Syrup (see recipe)
     ¼ cup falernum syrup*
         Ice cubes
      8 lime peel curls (optional)

Bring 2 cups water to boil in medium saucepan. Remove from heat. Mix in grated fresh ginger and 1 teaspoon lime juice. Cover and let stand 1 hour. Add brown sugar; stir to dissolve. Strain into bowl, pressing firmly on solids to extract as much liquid as possible (mixture will be cloudy). Cool completely. Transfer ginger liquid to jar. Cover and chill at least 2 hours or up to 1 week.

Mix rum, Simple Syrup, falernum syrup, ginger liquid, and remaining ¾ cup lime juice in pitcher. Fill tall glasses with ice. Pour mixture over. If desired, garnish rim of each glass with lime peel curl and serve.

Falernum syrup is a sweet syrup flavored with lime, almond, ginger, and spices that's used to sweeten drinks. It's available at some liquor stores and specialty foods stores.

8 SERVINGS

Aqua Pearl

     ¾ cup soursop (guanabana) juice* or pineapple juice
      6 tablespoons gin
      4 teaspoons fresh lemon juice
      4 teaspoons Simple Syrup (see recipe)
    1½ teaspoons blue curaçao liqueur
      4 dashes of angostura bitters
         Ice cubes
      2 unsprayed purple orchids (optional)

Mix first 6 ingredients in cocktail shaker. Fill with ice. Cover and shake well. Strain into 2 Daiquiri or Martini glasses. Garnish each with orchid, if desired, and serve.

Soursop (guanabana) juice is similar to pineapple juice and is sold at Latin markets nationwide.

2 SERVINGS

Pisco Punch

1 4-pound pineapple, peeled, cut into
    1-inch pieces
1 750-ml bottle Pisco
2 cups Simple Syrup (see recipe)
1½ teaspoons grated lime peel
1½ teaspoons grated white grapefruit
    peel

⅔ cup fresh lemon juice
   Ice cubes
12 pineapple leaves (optional)

Place pineapple pieces in large jar. Pour Pisco over. Cover and refrigerate 3 days, shaking occasionally. Divide Simple Syrup between 2 bowls. Mix grated lime peel into 1 bowl and grated grapefruit peel into the other. Cover and refrigerate both syrups overnight.

Strain Pisco into pitcher; discard pineapple pieces.

Strain both syrups into Pisco. Add lemon juice; stir to blend. Fill 12 small glasses with ice, then add punch. Garnish with pineapple leaves, if desired.

12 SERVINGS

Simple Syrup

1½ cups sugar
1½ cups water

Combine sugar and water in heavy large saucepan over medium heat until sugar dissolves. Increase heat and boil 3 minutes. Cool syrup, then cover and chill until cold, about 2 hours. (*Can be prepared 1 month ahead.*)

MAKES 2 CUPS

A Caribbean spin on the 100-year-old classic drink, this version infuses pineapple into Pisco (a South American brandy) and uses fresh grapefruit and lime peel for extra brightness.

Cucumber Gimlets

>   2   large cucumbers (1½ pounds total)
>
>   ½   cup gin
>   4   teaspoons fresh lime juice
>   1   tablespoon sugar
>   1   cup ice cubes
>   4   lime slices

Slice four ¼-inch-thick slices from 1 cucumber. Peel and coarsely chop remaining cucumbers; transfer to processor and puree until smooth. Pour through fine strainer set over large bowl, pressing on solids in strainer. Discard solids in strainer.

Mix 1 cup cucumber juice, gin, lime juice, and sugar in pitcher; stir until sugar dissolves. Add ice; mix well. Immediately strain mixture into 4 small Martini glasses. Garnish with lime and cucumber slices.

MAKES 4

Hot Orange Mocha with Grand Marnier Whipped Cream

>   ½   cup chilled whipping cream
>   2   tablespoons brown sugar, divided
>   1   tablespoon Grand Marnier or other orange liqueur
>
>   2   oranges
>   4   cups whole milk
>   6   ounces bittersweet (not unsweetened) chocolate, chopped
>   3   tablespoons instant espresso powder
>   1   tablespoon unsweetened cocoa powder
>   Ground coffee beans (optional)

Whisk cream, 1 tablespoon sugar, and Grand Marnier in medium bowl to soft peaks; cover and chill.

Using vegetable peeler, remove peel from oranges in strips; add strips to medium saucepan (reserve oranges for another use). Add milk; bring just to simmer over medium heat. Add chocolate, espresso powder, cocoa powder, and remaining 1 tablespoon sugar; bring just to simmer, whisking to melt chocolate. Strain. Ladle mocha into 4 mugs. Top with whipped cream and ground coffee beans, if desired.

4 SERVINGS

Après-Ski Lunch for 4

Hot Orange Mocha with Grand Marnier Whipped Cream
(at left)

Black Bean Chili with Butternut Squash and Swiss Chard
(page 104)

Tangy Avocado-Orange Salad
(page 145)

French Baguette

Beer and *Lemonade*

Cherry-Almond Clafouti
(page 213)

Coffee

Shrimp and Peppers with Spicy Rice (page 96)

Main Courses

Meats

Poultry

Seafood

Meatless

Pasta & Pizza

Grilled Steak with Fresh Garden Herbs

¼ cup minced shallots (about 2)

3 tablespoons fresh lemon juice

1 tablespoon red wine vinegar

1 teaspoon Dijon mustard

¼ cup extra-virgin olive oil plus additional for brushing

¾ cup assorted chopped fresh herbs (such as parsley, tarragon, mint, basil, and cilantro)

4 8-ounce rib-eye or skirt steaks

Whisk first 4 ingredients in medium bowl. Gradually whisk in ¼ cup olive oil, then herbs.

Prepare barbecue (medium-high heat). Sprinkle steaks generously with salt and pepper; brush lightly with olive oil. Grill steaks until charred and cooked to desired doneness, about 6 minutes per side for medium-rare rib-eye or 3 minutes per side for medium-rare skirt steak. Transfer steaks to platter; let rest 5 minutes. Spoon herb mixture over steaks; serve.

4 SERVINGS

Red-Wine Pot Roast with Porcini

1 cup low-salt chicken broth or beef broth

½ ounce dried porcini mushrooms

1 4-pound boneless beef chuck roast, trimmed

2 tablespoons extra-virgin olive oil

1 large onion, coarsely chopped

2 celery stalks with some leaves, cut into ½-inch-thick slices

3 garlic cloves, smashed

1 tablespoon chopped fresh marjoram plus sprigs for garnish

1 28-ounce can whole peeled tomatoes, drained

1 cup dry red wine

Preheat oven to 300°F. Bring broth to simmer in saucepan. Remove from heat; add mushrooms, cover, and let stand until soft, about 15 minutes. Using slotted spoon, transfer mushrooms to cutting board. Chop coarsely. Reserve mushrooms and broth separately.

Sprinkle beef with salt and pepper. Heat oil in heavy large ovenproof pot over medium-high heat. Add beef and cook until brown on all sides, about 15 minutes total. Transfer beef to large plate. Pour off all but 1 tablespoon drippings from pot. Place pot over medium heat. Add onion and celery. Sprinkle with salt and pepper and sauté until beginning to brown, about 8 minutes. Add garlic, chopped marjoram, and reserved porcini mushrooms;

MEATS

sauté 1 minute. Using hands, crush tomatoes, 1 at a time, into pot. Cook 3 minutes, stirring frequently and scraping up browned bits from bottom of pot. Add wine; boil 5 minutes. Add reserved mushroom broth, leaving any sediment behind. Boil 5 minutes.

Return beef and any accumulated juices to pot. Cover; transfer to oven. Cook 1½ hours. Turn beef and continue cooking until tender, about 1½ hours longer. *(Can be made 2 days ahead. Cool slightly. Refrigerate uncovered until cool. Cover and keep refrigerated.)*

Transfer beef to cutting board; tent with foil. Spoon fat from surface of juices in pot. Bring juices to boil; cook until liquid is reduced to 4 cups, about 7 minutes. Season with salt and pepper.

Cut beef into ½-inch-thick slices. Transfer to platter. Spoon juices over, garnish with marjoram sprigs, and serve.

6 SERVINGS

Sunday Family Supper for 6

Stuffed Mushrooms

Red-Wine Pot Roast with Porcini
(opposite; pictured at left)

Fennel Mashed Potatoes
(page 134)

Green Bean and Radish Salad
(page 145)

Zinfandel

Almond, Apricot, and Cream Cheese Crostata
(page 177)

Roasted Pancetta-Topped Beef Tenderloin with Wild Mushrooms

BEEF

    2 large garlic cloves, minced
    1 tablespoon minced fresh thyme
    1 tablespoon minced fresh rosemary
    1 large shallot, minced
    1 2¼-pound beef tenderloin roast
    2 3-ounce packages (about) thinly sliced pancetta (Italian bacon)

MUSHROOMS

    12 ounces fresh oyster mushrooms
    12 ounces fresh shiitake mushrooms, stemmed, halved
    ¼ cup olive oil
    ¼ cup finely chopped shallots
    2 garlic cloves, chopped
    1 tablespoon chopped fresh thyme
    1 tablespoon chopped fresh rosemary

    ¾ cup beef broth
    3 tablespoons brandy
    1 tablespoon chilled butter

FOR BEEF: Mix garlic, thyme, rosemary, and shallot in small bowl. Sprinkle beef with salt and pepper; rub herb mixture over. Place beef in roasting pan. Overlap pancetta slices atop beef to cover. (*Can be prepared 1 day ahead. Cover; chill.*)

FOR MUSHROOMS: Mix mushrooms, olive oil, shallots, garlic, and fresh herbs in large bowl.

Preheat oven to 450°F. Roast beef 15 minutes. Arrange mushroom mixture in pan around beef; roast 15 minutes. Stir mushrooms; continue to roast until thermometer inserted into beef from top center registers 125°F to 130°F for medium-rare, about 10 minutes. Transfer beef to platter; surround with mushroom mixture. Let rest 15 minutes.

Meanwhile, place roasting pan across 2 burners. Add broth and brandy; bring to boil, scraping up browned bits. Remove from heat. Whisk in cold butter. Season pan juices with salt and pepper. Transfer to bowl and serve with beef.

6 SERVINGS

Birthday Dinner for 6

Oysters on the Half Shell

Shrimp Cocktail

Pinot Gris

Roasted Pancetta-Topped
Beef Tenderloin with
Wild Mushrooms
(*at left; pictured opposite*)

Mashed Potatoes

Sautéed Spinach

Cabernet Sauvignon

Semisweet Chocolate
Layer Cake with
Vanilla Cream Filling
(*page 196*)

Cognac

Char-Grilled Beef-Tenderloin with Three-Herb Chimichurri Sauce

SPICE RUB

- 2 tablespoons dark brown sugar
- 1 tablespoon sweet smoked paprika*
- 1 tablespoon coarse kosher salt
- 1½ teaspoons chipotle chile powder or ancho chile powder
- 1 teaspoon ground black pepper

CHIMICHURRI SAUCE

- ¾ cup olive oil
- 3 tablespoons Sherry wine vinegar or red wine vinegar
- 3 tablespoons fresh lemon juice
- 3 garlic cloves, peeled
- 2 medium shallots, peeled, quartered
- 1 teaspoon fine sea salt
- ½ teaspoon freshly ground black pepper
- ½ teaspoon dried crushed red pepper
- 3 cups (packed) stemmed fresh parsley
- 2 cups (packed) stemmed fresh cilantro
- 1 cup (packed) stemmed fresh mint

BEEF TENDERLOIN

- 1 3½-pound beef tenderloin
- 2 tablespoons olive oil

FOR SPICE RUB: Combine all ingredients in small bowl. (*Can be made 2 days ahead. Store airtight at room temperature.*)

FOR CHIMICHURRI SAUCE: Combine first 8 ingredients in blender; blend until almost smooth. Add ¼ of parsley, ¼ of cilantro, and ¼ of mint; blend until incorporated. Add remaining herbs in 3 more additions, pureeing until almost smooth after each addition. (*Can be made 3 hours ahead. Cover; chill.*)

FOR BEEF TENDERLOIN: Let beef stand at room temperature 1 hour. Prepare barbecue (high heat). Pat beef dry with paper towels; brush with oil. Sprinkle all over with spice rub, using all of mixture (coating will be thick). Place beef on grill; sear 2 minutes on each side. Reduce heat to medium-high. Grill uncovered until instant-read thermometer inserted into thickest part of beef registers 130°F for medium-rare, moving beef to cooler part of grill as needed to prevent burning, and turning occasionally, about 40 minutes. Transfer to platter; cover loosely with foil and let rest 15 minutes. Slice and serve with chimichurri sauce.

Available at specialty foods stores.

8 TO 10 SERVINGS

Harissa-Crusted Tri-Tip Roast

1¾ teaspoons caraway seeds
¼ cup extra-virgin olive oil
6 garlic cloves
¼ cup chili paste (such as sambal oelek)*
2 tablespoons tomato sauce
1½ teaspoons ground cumin
1¼ teaspoons chili powder

1 1¾- to 2-pound tri-tip beef roast, most of fat layer trimmed

Harissa, a spicy North African chili-garlic condiment, can be found at some specialty foods stores and Middle Eastern markets. But it is very easy to make, too, as in this recipe.

Preheat oven to 400°F. Toast caraway seeds in small nonstick skillet over medium heat until seeds darken and begin to smoke, stirring often, about 5 minutes. Add olive oil and garlic cloves to caraway seeds in skillet. Cover; remove from heat. Let stand 1 minute. Pour caraway mixture into processor. Add chili paste, tomato sauce, cumin, and chili powder and blend until garlic cloves are pureed. Season harissa to taste with salt.

Sprinkle beef all over with salt and pepper; place beef, fat side down, on rack on rimmed baking sheet. Spread with half of harissa. Turn beef over; spread remaining harissa over top and sides. Roast beef until thermometer inserted into center registers 125°F to 130°F for medium-rare, about 35 minutes. Let rest 10 minutes. Slice and serve.

Available in the Asian foods section of most supermarkets and at Asian markets.

4 TO 6 SERVINGS

Braised Short Ribs with Chocolate and Rosemary

¼ cup diced pancetta (Italian bacon; about 1½ ounces)
6 pounds bone-in short ribs
1½ cups finely chopped onions
¼ cup finely chopped shallots
¼ cup finely chopped celery
¼ cup finely chopped peeled carrots
3 garlic cloves, minced
2 cups dry red wine
3 cups low-salt chicken broth
2 cups chopped drained canned diced tomatoes
2 tablespoons chopped fresh parsley
1 very large fresh thyme sprig
1 bay leaf

3 tablespoons shaved or grated bittersweet chocolate
2 tablespoons unsweetened cocoa powder (preferably Dutch-process)
1 teaspoon finely chopped fresh rosemary

Braised short ribs get deeper richness with the surprising addition of chocolate. Team this tender and flavorful dish with mashed potatoes and a Cabernet Sauvignon.

Heat heavy large pot over medium heat. Add pancetta and sauté until crisp. Using slotted spoon, transfer pancetta to paper towels to drain. Sprinkle ribs with salt and pepper. Working in batches, brown ribs in drippings in pot over medium-high heat until brown on all sides, about 8 minutes per batch. Transfer to plate. Add onions and next 4 ingredients to pot. Cover, reduce heat to medium, and cook until vegetables are soft, stirring occasionally, about 10 minutes. Add wine. Boil uncovered until liquid is reduced by half, scraping up browned bits, about 5 minutes. Add broth, tomatoes, parsley, thyme, bay leaf, and pancetta. Return ribs to pot, cover partially, and simmer 1½ hours. Uncover and simmer until rib meat is tender, stirring occasionally, about 1½ hours longer.

Transfer ribs to plate; discard bay leaf. Spoon fat from surface of sauce. Boil sauce until beginning to thicken, about 8 minutes. Reduce heat to medium. Add chocolate, cocoa powder, and rosemary; stir until chocolate melts. Season to taste with salt and pepper. Return ribs to pot. Simmer to rewarm, about 5 minutes.

6 TO 8 SERVINGS

Pepper-Crusted Beef, Bacon, and Arugula Sandwiches with Horseradish-Mustard Dressing

- 3 8-ounce beef tenderloin steaks
- 3 tablespoons coarsely cracked black peppercorns
- 6 tablespoons mayonnaise
- 2 tablespoons spicy Dijon mustard
- 1 tablespoon prepared white horseradish, drained

- 12 mushrooms, thinly sliced
- 6 tablespoons fresh lemon juice
  Olive oil
- 1 pound sliced bacon

- 6 3- to 4-inch-diameter kaiser, egg, or country-style rolls, cut in half horizontally, toasted if desired
- 3 cups (packed) baby arugula

Coat steaks all over with pepper. Mix mayonnaise, mustard, and horseradish in small bowl for dressing. Cover steaks and dressing separately and refrigerate at least 30 minutes and up to 1 day.

Toss mushrooms and lemon juice in medium bowl to coat evenly. Sprinkle lightly with salt. Brush heavy large skillet generously with oil and heat over medium-high heat. Add steaks and cook to desired doneness, about 5 minutes per side for medium-rare. Transfer steaks to plate; let stand 15 minutes. Cook bacon in same skillet over medium-high heat until brown and crisp. Using tongs, transfer bacon to paper towels to drain.

Place roll bottoms on plates; spread with dressing. Slice steaks thinly and divide among rolls. Top with bacon, mushrooms, and arugula. Cover sandwiches with roll tops and serve.

6 SERVINGS

Moroccan Beef Stew

- 3 tablespoons olive oil, divided
- 1¾ pounds beef tenderloin, cut into1-inch cubes
- 1 large onion, chopped
- 1 large carrot, chopped
- 2 garlic cloves, chopped
- 1 tablespoon paprika
- 2 teaspoons ground cumin
- 1½ teaspoons ground cinnamon
- 2 cups beef broth
- 1 15-ounce can garbanzo beans (chickpeas), drained
- ½ cup halved pitted Kalamata olives
- ½ cup golden raisins
- ½ cup chopped fresh cilantro
- 1 teaspoon finely grated lemon peel

Heat 2 tablespoons oil in heavy large pot over medium-high heat. Sprinkle beef with salt and pepper. Working in batches, add beef to pot and brown on all sides, about 3 minutes per batch. Transfer to plate. Add 1 tablespoon oil, onion, carrot, and garlic to pot. Cook until vegetables are soft, stirring often, about 10 minutes. Add spices; stir 1 minute. Add broth and next 4 ingredients; bring to boil. Simmer until juices thicken, about 5 minutes. Add beef and any accumulated juices and lemon peel to pot. Stir until warm and serve.

6 SERVINGS

North African Dinner for 6

Fresh Figs with Goat Cheese and Peppered Honey
(page 18)

Moroccan Beef Stew
(at left; pictured at left)

Couscous

Arugula Salad

Cabernet Franc

Walnuts, Dates, and Orange Wedges

Tea

Grilled Steak and Onions with Rosemary-Balsamic Butter Sauce

8 tablespoons (1 stick) chilled unsalted butter, divided
1 large shallot, minced
½ cup balsamic vinegar
2 large fresh rosemary sprigs

2 pounds mixed sweet onions, large shallots, baby leeks, and green onions
2 tablespoons olive oil

4 1¼-inch-thick New York strip steaks (each about 6 ounces)

2 tablespoons orange juice

Melt 6 tablespoons butter in heavy small saucepan over medium heat. Add minced shallot and cook until translucent, about 2 minutes. Add vinegar and rosemary and simmer until syrupy and reduced to ½ cup, about 6 minutes. Remove from heat (balsamic sauce will separate as it stands).

Prepare barbecue (medium-high heat). Peel sweet onions, then cut into ½-inch-thick rounds. Skewer horizontally with toothpicks to keep intact. Peel shallots; cut in half lengthwise. Trim root ends and tops of leeks. Cut in half lengthwise; rinse to remove any dirt. Trim root ends of green onions. Place sweet onions, shallots, leeks, and green onions on rimmed baking sheet and drizzle with oil; toss. Sprinkle with salt and pepper.

Sprinkle steaks with salt and pepper. Grill sweet onions, shallots, leeks, and green onions until tender, turning often, about 5 minutes for green onions and 10 minutes for sweet onions, shallots, and leeks. Move onions to cooler part of grill to keep warm. Grill steaks to desired doneness, about 7 minutes per side for medium-rare. Transfer steaks and onions to platter; cover.

Remove rosemary sprigs from balsamic sauce; add orange juice and bring to simmer. Remove saucepan from heat; add remaining 2 tablespoons chilled butter and whisk until melted and sauce is smooth. Season sauce to taste with salt and pepper. Drizzle some of sauce over steaks and onions. Serve, passing remaining sauce separately.

4 SERVINGS

Salt-Roasted Porterhouse

    3 bay leaves, crushed
    1 tablespoon whole black peppercorns
    2 teaspoons whole coriander seeds
    2 teaspoons fennel seeds
    2 teaspoons mustard seeds
    2 teaspoons dried rosemary
  ½ teaspoon dried crushed red pepper
    1 teaspoon plus 1½ cups coarse kosher salt
    1 30-ounce porterhouse or T-bone steak (about 2 to 2¼ inches thick)

  ¼ cup water

Although it seems that packing a steak in salt would cause it to dry out and taste too salty, this coating of coarse salt serves as a barrier, keeping moisture in. The result? A juicy, flavorful steak to dream about.

Mix first 7 ingredients in small bowl. Transfer 2 tablespoons spice mixture to spice grinder; grind finely. Mix in 1 teaspoon salt. *(Can be made 1 week ahead. Store whole and ground spice mixtures separately in airtight containers at room temperature.)* Rub ground spice mixture all over steak. Wrap in plastic; chill 3 hours.

Preheat oven to 475°F. Unwrap steak; place in large ovenproof skillet. Mix whole spice mixture with 1½ cups kosher salt in medium bowl. Add ¼ cup water; stir to moisten. Pack salt over top and sides of steak. Roast until instant-read thermometer inserted horizontally into steak registers 130°F for medium-rare, about 25 minutes. Let stand at room temperature 8 minutes. Crack salt crust with wooden spoon; discard. Turn steak over. Slice into ½-inch-thick slices.

2 SERVINGS

Braised Lamb Shanks with Coriander, Fennel, and Star Anise

2 tablespoons coriander seeds
2 tablespoons fennel seeds
1 tablespoon black peppercorns
4 large lamb shanks (about 5 pounds)

4 tablespoons olive oil, divided
1 large white onion, cut into 1½-inch pieces
10 garlic cloves, peeled
3 celery stalks, cut crosswise into 1½-inch pieces
2 carrots, peeled, cut crosswise into 1½-inch pieces
1 small leek, white and pale green parts only, cut crosswise into 1½-inch pieces
3 cups ruby Port
4 cups low-salt chicken broth
4 cups beef broth

6 whole cloves
2 whole star anise*
2 bay leaves
½ teaspoon dried crushed red pepper

Mix coriander, fennel, and peppercorns in heavy small skillet. Toast on medium-high heat until aromatic and slightly darker, about 2 minutes. Transfer to spice grinder; process until finely ground. Rub each shank with 1 rounded teaspoon spice blend. Sprinkle with salt and pepper.

Heat 2 tablespoons oil in heavy large wide pot over medium-high heat. Add shanks to pot. Cook until brown on all sides, about 20 minutes. Transfer to large bowl. Add remaining 2 tablespoons oil to same pot. Add onion and next 4 ingredients; sauté over medium heat until vegetables begin to soften, about 5 minutes. Add remaining spice blend and stir 1 minute. Add Port and simmer until liquid is reduced to ⅔ cup, about 15 minutes. Add both broths; boil until liquid is reduced to 3½ cups, about 30 minutes.

Preheat oven to 350°F. Return shanks to pot. Add cloves, star anise, bay leaves, and crushed red pepper. Cover pot with foil, then lid. Place pot in oven and braise lamb until tender, about 2 hours. (Can be made 2 days ahead. Uncover and cool slightly. Place in refrigerator until cool, then cover and keep refrigerated. Rewarm in 350°F oven for 20 minutes before serving.)

Place 1 lamb shank on each of 4 plates. Season sauce to taste with salt and pepper. Spoon sauce and vegetables over lamb and serve.

*Brown, star-shaped seed pods; available in the spice section of some supermarkets, at Asian markets, and at specialty foods stores.

4 SERVINGS

Lamb Stew with Leeks and Baby Artichokes

3½	pounds boneless lamb shoulder meat, trimmed of excess fat, cut into 2-inch pieces
1¼	cups chopped fresh Italian parsley
3	garlic cloves, minced
1	tablespoon finely grated lemon peel
3	tablespoons olive oil
2	large leeks (white and pale green parts only), thinly sliced (about 2½ cups)
1	large onion, thinly sliced
¾	teaspoon dried thyme
1½	cups (or more) low-salt chicken broth
½	lemon
18	baby artichokes (about 1¾ pounds)
	Rice

Place trimmed lamb in large bowl; sprinkle generously with salt and pepper. Cover and let stand at room temperature 30 minutes.

Combine 1 cup chopped parsley, minced garlic, and grated lemon peel in small bowl. Reserve remaining ¼ cup parsley for garnish.

Heat oil in heavy large pot over high heat. Working in batches, add lamb and cook until well browned on all sides, about 7 minutes per batch. Transfer lamb to medium bowl. Add leeks and onion to drippings in pot and sauté until softened, about 7 minutes. Add chopped parsley mixture and thyme; stir 30 seconds. Return lamb and any accumulated juices to pot. Add 1½ cups broth and bring to boil. Reduce heat to medium-low; cover and simmer until lamb is very tender, about 1½ hours. (*Lamb stew can be prepared 1 day ahead of serving. Cool slightly. Refrigerate stew uncovered until cold, then cover and keep refrigerated. Bring lamb stew to simmer before continuing with recipe.*)

Fill medium bowl with cold water. Squeeze juice from lemon half into water; add squeezed lemon half. Break off tough outer leaves from 1 artichoke where leaves break naturally, stopping when first yellow leaves are reached. Cut off stem and top ½ inch from artichoke, then cut artichoke in half lengthwise and drop into lemon water. Repeat with remaining artichokes.

Drain artichokes and add to lamb stew. Bring to boil. Reduce heat to medium-low; cover and simmer until artichokes are tender, adding more broth by ¼ cupfuls if stew is dry, about 25 minutes. Season stew to taste with salt and pepper. Transfer to bowl; sprinkle lamb stew with reserved ¼ cup chopped parsley and serve with rice.

6 SERVINGS

Hoisin-Orange Roast Rack of Lamb with Red Onions

Olive oil
2   1²/₃-pound racks of lamb, well trimmed
2   medium-size red onions, cut through root ends into ½-inch-thick wedges
½   cup hoisin sauce*
¼   cup frozen orange juice concentrate
1½ tablespoons minced peeled fresh ginger
1   tablespoon chili-garlic sauce*
¾   teaspoon Chinese five-spice powder** or ground aniseed

Preheat oven to 450°F. Brush large rimmed baking sheet with olive oil. Place lamb racks in center of baking sheet. Arrange onion wedges around lamb. Brush lamb and onion wedges with olive oil. Whisk hoisin, orange juice concentrate, minced ginger, chili-garlic sauce, and Chinese five-spice powder in small bowl to blend. Brush hoisin glaze generously over lamb and onion wedges; sprinkle with salt and generous amount of pepper.

Roast until instant-read thermometer inserted into lamb registers 130°F for medium-rare, about 25 minutes. Transfer lamb racks to plate. Continue roasting onion wedges until tender, about 5 minutes longer. Divide onion wedges among plates. Cut lamb racks into chops; place lamb atop onion wedges and serve.

*Available in the Asian foods section of many supermarkets and at Asian markets.
**Chinese five-spice powder may contain ground aniseed, fennel seeds, Szechuan peppercorns, cinnamon, star anise, cloves, or ginger; it can be found in the spice section of most supermarkets.

4 SERVINGS

Roast Leg of Lamb with Salsa Verde

1   cup extra-virgin olive oil
½   cup fresh lemon juice
½   cup chopped fresh Italian parsley
²/₃ cup finely chopped green onions
¼   cup chopped fresh mint
¼   cup salted capers, soaked in cold water 30 minutes, or brined capers, drained, chopped
1   tablespoon grated lemon peel
1   teaspoon salt
½   teaspoon dried crushed red pepper
½   teaspoon ground black pepper
1   5½-pound boneless leg of lamb, butterflied, trimmed
1   tablespoon minced garlic

Stir first 10 ingredients in large bowl for salsa verde. Place lamb on work surface, smooth side down. Sprinkle lamb with salt and pepper, then garlic. Rub ¼ cup salsa verde into lamb. Roll up lamb. Using kitchen string, tie lamb every 2 inches to hold together. (*Lamb and salsa verde can be prepared 1 day ahead. Cover separately and chill.*)

Preheat oven to 450°F. Place lamb on rack in roasting pan. Roast until thermometer inserted into thickest part of lamb registers 125°F for medium-rare, about 1 hour 20 minutes. Let stand at room temperature 15 minutes. Transfer lamb to cutting board; remove kitchen string. Cut lamb crosswise into thin slices. Arrange on platter. Spoon some salsa verde over. Serve lamb, passing remaining salsa alongside.

8 SERVINGS

Have the butcher trim and butterfly the leg of lamb. Round out the menu with rice pilaf and roasted fennel.

Minted Lamb Burgers with Feta and Hummus

1½	pounds ground lamb
½	cup minced fresh mint
2	garlic cloves, pressed
1	tablespoon paprika
1	teaspoon salt
½	teaspoon cayenne pepper
¼	teaspoon cinnamon
1	tablespoon olive oil
1	7- to 8-ounce block feta cheese, sliced
4	kaiser rolls, split, lightly toasted
8	onion slices
4	romaine lettuce leaves
	Purchased hummus

Mix first 7 ingredients in medium bowl; shape into four 4-inch-diameter patties. Heat olive oil in heavy large skillet over medium-high heat. Add patties to skillet; cook until bottoms are well browned, about 3 minutes. Turn patties over and top with feta cheese. Continue cooking to desired doneness, about 3 minutes longer for medium-rare.

Place roll bottoms on plates. Top each with onion, burger, lettuce, another onion, and hummus. Press on roll tops.

4 SERVINGS

Lamb Stew with Lemon and Figs

1½ cups plain whole-milk yogurt
3 tablespoons chopped fresh mint

½ cup warm water
¼ teaspoon saffron threads, crumbled

1 2½- to 3-pound boneless lamb shoulder, trimmed, cut into 1- to 1½-inch cubes
2 tablespoons (or more) olive oil
2 onions (about 1 pound), thinly sliced
1 small lemon (preferably Meyer), ends trimmed, quartered lengthwise, thinly sliced crosswise
4 garlic cloves, minced
1 rounded teaspoon minced peeled fresh ginger
¼ teaspoon ground cinnamon
⅛ teaspoon cayenne pepper
1 14½-ounce can diced tomatoes in juice
1 cup dried figs, stems trimmed, quartered lengthwise (about 4 ounces)
2½ cups (or more) low-salt chicken broth

Crispy Noodle Cake (see recipe)

Set strainer lined with double layer of cheesecloth over medium bowl. Place yogurt in strainer; cover and chill 3 to 5 hours to drain. Transfer yogurt to small bowl. Stir in mint; season with salt and pepper. *(Can be made 1 day ahead. Chill.)*

Place ½ cup warm water and saffron in small bowl; let stand 20 minutes to infuse.

Sprinkle lamb with salt and pepper. Heat 2 tablespoons oil in heavy large pot over medium-high heat. Working in batches, cook lamb until brown on all sides, adding more oil as needed, about 5 minutes per batch. Transfer lamb to large bowl. Pour all but 1 tablespoon fat from pot (or add 1 tablespoon oil if dry); heat pot over medium heat. Add onions; sprinkle with salt and pepper. Sauté until beginning to brown, about 5 minutes. Add lemon, garlic, ginger, cinnamon, and cayenne. Stir 1 minute. Add saffron mixture; stir, scraping up browned bits. Add tomatoes with juice, figs, and lamb with any juices to pot. Stir to coat. Add 2½ cups broth.

Bring stew to boil. Reduce heat to medium-low, then cover with lid slightly ajar and simmer until meat is tender, stirring occasionally and adding more broth by ¼ cupfuls as needed if dry, about 1½ hours. Season to taste with salt and pepper. *(Can be made 2 days ahead. Cool slightly. Refrigerate uncovered until cold, then cover and chill.)*

Bring stew to simmer, thinning with more chicken broth if necessary. Divide stew among 6 plates; top each serving with dollop of minted yogurt. Place wedge of Crispy Noodle Cake alongside each and serve.

6 SERVINGS

Crispy Noodle Cake

12	ounces fresh linguine
3	tablespoons extra-virgin olive oil, divided
¼	cup chopped fresh Italian parsley

Cook pasta in large pot of boiling salted water until tender but still firm to bite, stirring occasionally. Drain. Transfer pasta to medium bowl; toss with 1 tablespoon oil and parsley. Season generously with salt and pepper. *(Can be prepared 1 hour ahead. Let pasta stand at room temperature, tossing occasionally.)*

Lightly oil large plate. Heat 1 tablespoon oil in heavy medium skillet over medium heat. Add pasta to skillet, spreading evenly, flattening top, and pressing down with spatula to compress. Cook until brown and crisp, about 3 minutes. Carefully invert cake onto prepared plate. Return skillet to medium heat. Add remaining 1 tablespoon oil. Slide noodle cake into skillet and cook until brown and crisp on bottom, about 3 minutes. Transfer cake to cutting board, cut into wedges, and serve.

6 SERVINGS

Grilled Pork Chops with Maple-Cranberry Glaze

SPICE RUB

- 1 tablespoon sugar
- 1 tablespoon hot smoked paprika (Pimentón de la Vera)*
- 2 teaspoons seasoned salt
- 2 teaspoons dry mustard
- 2 teaspoons fine sea salt
- 2 teaspoons celery salt
- 2 teaspoons garlic salt
- 2 teaspoons ground black pepper
- 1 teaspoon onion powder
- 1 teaspoon ground chipotle chile powder or ancho chile powder

GLAZE

- ¾ cup jellied cranberry sauce (about half of one 16-ounce can)
- ½ cup pure maple syrup
- ¼ cup cran-raspberry juice
- 2 tablespoons Dijon mustard
- 1 tablespoon triple sec or other orange liqueur
- 1½ teaspoons grated orange peel
- ¼ teaspoon fine sea salt
- ¼ teaspoon ground black pepper

  Nonstick vegetable oil spray
- 8 ¾-inch-thick center-cut pork rib chops

FOR SPICE RUB: Mix all ingredients in small bowl.

FOR GLAZE: Mix first 8 ingredients in small saucepan. Bring to boil over medium heat, whisking until smooth. Cool to room temperature. (*Spice rub and glaze can be made 1 day ahead. Cover and store spice rub at room temperature. Cover and refrigerate glaze. Rewarm glaze just until pourable before using.*)

Spray grill rack with nonstick spray and prepare barbecue (medium heat). Sprinkle spice rub generously over both sides of pork chops (about ½ tablespoon per side), pressing to adhere. Place pork chops on grill, cover, and cook 5 minutes per side. Brush generously with glaze. Move to cooler part of grill and continue to grill, uncovered, until cooked through, brushing frequently with glaze, about 3 minutes longer per side.

Available at specialty foods stores.

8 SERVINGS

Summer Supper Under the Stars for 8

Beer-Battered Squash Blossoms
(*page 20*)

Grilled Pork Chops with Maple-Cranberry Glaze
(*at left; pictured opposite*)

Grilled Corn on the Cob

Caesar Salad

Zinfandel

Fresh Peach Ice Cream with Blackberries
(*page 220*)

Shortbread Cookies

Pancetta, Mizuna, and Tomato Sandwiches with Green Garlic Aioli

AIOLI

¼ cup extra-virgin olive oil

2 tablespoons chopped green garlic or 1 regular garlic clove, blanched

¼ teaspoon fleur de sel or coarse kosher salt

¾ cup mayonnaise, divided

2 teaspoons fresh lemon juice

SANDWICHES

2 3-ounce packages thinly sliced pancetta (Italian bacon; about 30 slices)

12 ½-inch-thick slices brioche or egg bread, lightly toasted

1 large bunch mizuna or arugula, torn into 2-inch pieces

3 beefsteak tomatoes, cut into ¼-inch-thick rounds

FOR AIOLI: Blend olive oil, garlic, and ¼ teaspoon fleur de sel in processor until garlic is minced. Add 2 tablespoons mayonnaise and blend well. Transfer to small bowl; whisk in remaining mayonnaise and lemon juice. (*Can be made 1 day ahead. Cover; chill.*)

FOR SANDWICHES: Preheat oven to 450°F. Arrange pancetta slices in single layer on 2 large rimmed baking sheets. Bake until crisp, about 10 minutes. Transfer to paper towels to drain.

Place toast on work surface. Spread with aioli. Divide mizuna among 6 toast slices; top with tomatoes, then pancetta, dividing equally. Top with remaining 6 toast slices, aioli side down. Cut each sandwich in half and serve.

MAKES 6

This may be the ultimate BLT. Look for mizuna, a feathery delicate salad green at farmers' markets and Asian markets. Green garlic, sometimes available at farmers' markets, resembles baby leeks with long green tops and white bulbs sometimes tinged with pink. It's much milder in flavor than regular garlic.

Grilled Sausages and Citrus with Herb-Marinated Onions

½ cup extra-virgin olive oil
4 large fresh basil leaves plus more for garnish
3 garlic cloves, peeled
3 tablespoons fresh lemon juice
2 tablespoons chopped fresh Italian parsley plus whole sprigs for garnish
3 medium-size red onions, each cut into 8 wedges with some core attached to each wedge

3 lemons, unpeeled, halved
3 limes, unpeeled, halved
2 grapefruits, unpeeled, each cut into 8 wedges
12 fresh or smoked sausages (such as fresh Italian, andouille, or kielbasa)

Puree oil, 4 basil leaves, garlic, lemon juice, and 2 tablespoons parsley in blender. Season marinade with salt and pepper. Pour into large bowl. Add onions; toss. Let marinate at least 30 minutes and up to 2 hours, tossing occasionally.

Prepare barbecue (medium-high heat). Transfer onions to grill, reserving marinade in bowl. Grill onions until charred at edges, turning occasionally, about 15 minutes. Arrange on platter.

Add all fruit to reserved marinade; toss. Arrange fruit and sausages on grill. Cook until fruit is charred and sausages are cooked through, turning occasionally, 10 to 20 minutes (times for smoked fully cooked and fresh uncooked sausages will vary). Arrange sausages and fruit atop onions. Garnish with basil and parsley.

12 SERVINGS

Just a few minutes on the grill gives the lemons, limes, and grapefruit great flavor—and they're delicious paired with the smoky sausages. Have plenty of cold beer on hand to go with the sausages.

Bourbon-Glazed Baby Back Ribs

 5 tablespoons honey
 ¼ cup bourbon
 1½ tablespoons hoisin sauce*
 1 tablespoon Dijon mustard
 1 tablespoon plum sauce
 1½ teaspoons mild-flavored (light) molasses
 1½ teaspoons soy sauce
 1½ teaspoons Worcestershire sauce
 ¾ teaspoon hot chili paste (such as sambal oelek)**
 ¼ teaspoon salt
 ¼ teaspoon ground black pepper

 2 2¼- to 2½-pound racks baby back pork ribs
 1 cup unsweetened pineapple juice

Whisk first 11 ingredients in small bowl. (*Glaze can be made 1 day ahead. Cover and refrigerate.*)

Preheat oven to 350°F. Place long sheet of heavy-duty foil on each of 2 large rimmed baking sheets. Sprinkle rib racks on all sides with salt and pepper. Place 1 rib rack on each foil sheet. Fold up sides of each foil sheet around rib rack to form boat-like shape. Pour $1/2$ cup pineapple juice over each rib rack. Fold up foil to seal packets. Bake until ribs are tender, about 1 hour. Remove ribs from foil packets. Transfer to roasting pan; pour any juices from foil over and cool. (*Can be made 1 day ahead. Cover with plastic wrap; refrigerate.*)

Prepare barbecue (medium heat). Cut each rib rack in half. Grill until browned, brushing frequently with glaze and turning often, about 10 minutes. Cut racks between bones into ribs.

Sold in the Asian foods section of many supermarkets and at Asian markets.
**An Indonesian hot chili paste; available at many supermarkets and at Asian markets nationwide.*

6 SERVINGS

Bourbon adds oaky sweetness to the honey-hoisin-chili glaze.

Coke-Braised Pork Carnitas

4	pounds pork butt or pork shoulder (preferably Berkshire pork), trimmed, cut into 3x3-inch chunks
10¼	cups peanut oil, divided
4	cups orange juice
2½	cups cola-flavored soda, divided

Sprinkle pork with salt and pepper. Heat $1/4$ cup peanut oil in heavy 8-quart pot over high heat. Working in batches, add pork to pot and sauté until browned on all sides, about 7 minutes per batch. Using slotted spoon, transfer pork to large bowl.

Pour remaining 10 cups peanut oil into same pot. Attach deep-fry thermometer to side of pot; heat over medium heat until thermometer registers 280°F. Add pork to oil in pot (temperature of oil will drop to between 180°F and 200°F). Cook pork over medium heat until brown and tender, adjusting heat as necessary to maintain temperature of oil between 200°F and 220°F, about $1 1/2$ hours. Using slotted spoon, transfer pork to another large pot. Add orange juice and 2 cups cola to pork and bring to boil; reduce heat and simmer until pork is very tender, about 35 minutes. Add remaining $1/2$ cup cola and stir over medium heat until meat falls apart and liquid is absorbed, about 5 minutes longer. Season generously with salt and pepper. Transfer to bowl and serve.

6 TO 8 SERVINGS

Coke is the secret ingredient in these braised pork *carnitas*, giving them a fresh new spin. Slow-cooking in Coke makes the meat meltingly tender, thanks to the combination of braising and the phosphoric acid in cola, which acts as a tenderizer. That sweetness adds great flavor, too. Serve the *carnitas* with mashed sweet potatoes, mixed baby greens, or rolled up in warm tortillas with salsa, chopped onions, and cilantro. Be sure to keep the oil at moderate heat, which will cook the pork perfectly without overbrowning.

Roast Chicken with Maple-Soy Glaze

¼ cup pure maple syrup
1 tablespoon soy sauce
1 tablespoon rice vinegar
½ teaspoon hot pepper sauce
¾ cup dry Sherry

1 4½-pound chicken, fat and giblets removed, rinsed and patted dry
2 tablespoons (¼ stick) butter, room temperature
½ orange, cut into 4 pieces
2 ½-inch slices fresh ginger, smashed
2 garlic cloves, smashed

Preheat oven to 375°F. Whisk maple syrup, soy sauce, rice vinegar, and hot pepper sauce in small bowl for glaze. Simmer Sherry in small saucepan until reduced to ½ cup, about 3 minutes.

Run hands under chicken skin to loosen; rub most of butter under skin, over breast and thighs. Rub remaining butter over outside of chicken. Sprinkle cavity with salt and pepper. Place chicken in roasting pan. Squeeze some juice from each orange piece over chicken.

Stuff cavity with orange pieces, ginger, and garlic. Tuck wing tips under. Pour Sherry over chicken.

Roast chicken 20 minutes. Add ¼ cup water to pan. Roast 15 minutes longer. Brush chicken with glaze. Roast chicken until thermometer inserted into thickest part of thigh registers 170°F, brushing chicken with glaze every 10 minutes, about 40 minutes longer. Tilt chicken to allow juices from cavity to run into roasting pan. Transfer chicken to platter. Let stand 10 minutes (internal temperature will rise).

Spoon fat from surface of pan juices. Add any remaining glaze to pan juices. Place roasting pan over 2 burners; bring sauce to boil. Serve sauce alongside chicken.

4 SERVINGS

Pecan- and Panko-Crusted Chicken Breasts

      4 skinless boneless chicken breast halves
      1 cup panko (Japanese breadcrumbs)*
      1 cup finely chopped pecans
      6 tablespoons (¾ stick) butter, divided

      ¼ cup minced shallots
      ¾ cup low-salt chicken broth
      2 tablespoons chopped fresh parsley

Preheat oven to 400°F. Sprinkle chicken with salt and pepper. Mix panko and pecans in dish. Melt 4 tablespoons butter in heavy large ovenproof skillet over medium-high heat. Remove skillet from heat; brush some of melted butter onto chicken, then coat chicken in panko mixture. Place skillet over medium heat. Add chicken and sauté until brown on bottom, about 2 minutes. Turn chicken over. Place skillet in oven. Bake until chicken is cooked through, about 18 minutes. Transfer chicken to platter.

Using slotted spoon, remove any crumbs from skillet. Add remaining 2 tablespoons butter and shallots; sauté over medium-high heat 1 minute. Add broth and simmer until slightly reduced, about 1 minute. Mix in parsley. Season sauce with salt and pepper; drizzle over chicken.

Available in the Asian foods section of some supermarkets and at Asian markets.

4 SERVINGS

Dinner in the Kitchen for 4

Ginger-Garlic Hummus
(page 15)

Roast Chicken with Maple-Soy Glaze
(opposite; pictured opposite)

Green-Onion Risotto
(page 139)

Buttered Green Beans

Chardonnay

Chilled Lemon Soufflés with Caramel Sauce
(page 208)

Herb-Basted Chicken with Pearl Barley, Bacon, and Root Vegetable Pilaf

PILAF

- 2 cups water
- ½ teaspoon salt
- 1 cup pearl barley, rinsed, drained

- 6 ounces bacon, diced
- 1 shallot, minced
- 1¼ cups ¼- to ⅓-inch cubes peeled root vegetables (such as celery root, carrot, turnip, and/or rutabaga)
  Pinch of sugar
- 2 teaspoons fresh lemon juice
- ½ teaspoon chopped fresh thyme
- ½ teaspoon chopped fresh rosemary

CHICKEN

- 6 tablespoons canola oil
- 4 large chicken breast halves with skin and bones
- 2 tablespoons (¼ stick) butter
- ½ teaspoon chopped fresh thyme
- ½ teaspoon chopped fresh rosemary

FOR PILAF: Bring 2 cups water and salt to boil in medium saucepan. Mix in barley. Cover pan, reduce heat to medium, and simmer until barley is tender, about 30 minutes. Drain barley and set aside.

Sauté bacon in large pot over medium heat until brown and crisp. Using slotted spoon, transfer bacon to paper towels. Pour off all but 2 tablespoons drippings from pot. Add shallot; stir 30 seconds. Add cubed vegetables and sugar; sauté 6 minutes. Add barley, lemon juice, and herbs; stir 2 minutes. Mix in bacon; season with salt and pepper. (*Can be made 1 hour ahead. Let stand at room temperature. Cover and place in oven to rewarm while chicken roasts, adding water by tablespoonfuls to moisten if dry.*)

FOR CHICKEN: Preheat oven to 350°F. Heat oil in large ovenproof skillet over medium-high heat. Sprinkle chicken with salt and pepper. Place chicken, skin side down, in skillet. Cook until skin browns, about 7 minutes. Add butter and herbs to skillet; stir to blend. Turn chicken skin side up. Place skillet in oven; roast chicken until cooked through, basting occasionally with herb butter, about 20 minutes.

Divide pilaf among 4 plates; top with chicken. Spoon pan juices over.

4 SERVINGS

Roasted Spiced Chicken with Cinnamon- and Honey-Glazed Sweet Potatoes

CHICKEN

- ½ cup chopped onion
- 4 garlic cloves, chopped
- 3 tablespoons apple cider vinegar
- 2 tablespoons honey
- 1 tablespoon allspice berries, ground in spice mill or coffee grinder
- 1 tablespoon chopped peeled fresh ginger
- 1½ teaspoons finely chopped fresh thyme
- 1 teaspoon salt
- 1 teaspoon ground black pepper
- ½ Scotch bonnet chile or habanero chile, seeded, minced
- ½ teaspoon ground cinnamon
- ¼ teaspoon ground nutmeg
- 4 whole chicken leg-thigh pieces (about 2¼ to 2½ pounds)

- 2 tablespoons olive oil

SWEET POTATOES

- Nonstick vegetable oil spray
- 2 tablespoons (¼ stick) butter, melted
- 2 tablespoons honey
- 1 tablespoon fresh lime juice
- ½ teaspoon ground cinnamon
- 2 pounds red-skinned sweet potatoes (yams), peeled, cut into ⅓-inch-thick rounds
- Mango chutney

FOR CHICKEN: Place first 12 ingredients in processor. Puree marinade until coarse paste forms. Place chicken in large resealable plastic bag. Add marinade to chicken in bag and seal. Turn chicken to coat. Refrigerate at least 8 hours or overnight, turning chicken occasionally.

Preheat oven to 400°F. Arrange chicken pieces, with marinade still clinging to chicken, on rimmed baking sheet. Brush chicken with oil. Roast until cooked through, about 45 minutes.

MEANWHILE, FOR SWEET POTATOES: Spray another rimmed baking sheet with nonstick spray. Whisk butter, honey, lime juice, and ground cinnamon in large bowl. Add potato slices; toss to coat. Arrange potato slices in single layer on prepared baking sheet. Sprinkle with salt and pepper. Bake potatoes alongside chicken until tender, about 25 minutes. Serve chicken with potatoes, passing mango chutney separately.

4 SERVINGS

This dish makes delicious use of the warm spices prevalent throughout Caribbean cooking. The chicken needs time to marinate, so start the recipe ahead.

Chicken Breasts with Wild Mushrooms, Marjoram, and Marsala

4 large skinless boneless chicken breast halves
6 teaspoons chopped fresh marjoram, divided
2 tablespoons butter, divided
2 tablespoons olive oil, divided
12 ounces assorted wild mushrooms (such as oyster, stemmed shiitake, and baby bella), thickly sliced
1 cup sliced shallots (about 5)

¾ cup low-salt chicken broth
½ cup whipping cream
3 tablespoons dry Marsala

Sprinkle chicken breasts with salt and pepper, then 2 teaspoons marjoram. Melt 1 tablespoon butter with 1 tablespoon oil in large nonstick skillet over medium-high heat. Add chicken to skillet and sauté until just cooked through, about 7 minutes per side. Transfer chicken to plate; tent with foil to keep warm. Melt remaining 1 tablespoon butter with 1 tablespoon oil in same skillet. Add mushrooms, shallots, and 2 teaspoons marjoram. Sauté until mushrooms are brown and tender, about 6 minutes. Season to taste with salt and pepper. Transfer to bowl.

Combine broth, cream, Marsala, and remaining 2 teaspoons marjoram in same skillet; boil until thickened and reduced to ½ cup, about 5 minutes. Season sauce with salt and pepper.

Divide mushrooms among 4 plates. Top mushrooms with chicken. Spoon sauce over and serve.

4 SERVINGS

Achiote Chicken with Tangerine Sauce

      2 tablespoons achiote paste*
      1 tablespoon honey
      1 tablespoon red wine vinegar
      1 tablespoon grated tangerine peel
      2 garlic cloves
      1 teaspoon cumin seeds
    ½ teaspoon ground cinnamon
      4 skinless boneless chicken breast halves

      1 tablespoon olive oil
      1 cup fresh tangerine juice, divided
         Chopped fresh cilantro

Blend first 7 ingredients in processor to form paste. Place chicken in 8-inch square baking dish. Spread marinade over, turning to coat. Cover; refrigerate at least 2 hours and up to 4 hours.

Heat oil in large nonstick skillet over medium-high heat. Sprinkle chicken with salt. Add to skillet; cook until brown, about 2 minutes per side. Add ½ cup juice to skillet. Cover; reduce heat to medium and simmer until chicken is cooked through, turning once, about 5 minutes. Transfer chicken to plates. Add ½ cup juice to skillet; boil until thickened, about 2 minutes. Season with salt and pepper; spoon over chicken. Sprinkle with cilantro.

*Achiote paste is available at Latin markets.

4 SERVINGS

Mustard-Roasted Chicken

      1 cup Dijon mustard
    ¼ cup extra-virgin olive oil
    ¼ cup chopped fresh Italian parsley
      2 tablespoons fresh thyme leaves
    16 garlic cloves, peeled, crushed
      2 3½- to 4-pound whole chickens, rinsed, patted dry

      6 fresh rosemary sprigs
      6 fresh sage sprigs

Whisk mustard, olive oil, parsley, and thyme in small bowl to blend. Stir in garlic. Spread mustard mixture generously inside cavities and over outside of chickens. Place chickens in glass baking dish; cover and refrigerate at least 4 hours or overnight.

Let chickens stand at room temperature 30 minutes. Sprinkle chickens generously inside and out with salt and pepper; let chickens stand 30 minutes longer.

Preheat oven to 400°F. Place chickens on rack set in large roasting pan. Tie legs together to hold shape. Spread any accumulated mustard marinade from dish over chickens. Place rosemary and sage sprigs atop chickens. Roast chickens until juices run clear when fork is inserted into thickest part of thigh, basting occasionally with pan juices, about 1 hour 10 minutes.

Carve chickens and arrange on platter. Spoon some of pan juices over and serve.

6 SERVINGS

The chicken needs to marinate for at least four hours (or overnight), so be sure to start in advance. Serve with roast potatoes, sautéed spinach, and a crisp, full-bodied white like Chablis or an unoaked California Chardonnay.

Sautéed Chicken Breasts with Country Ham and Summer Succotash

  5 tablespoons extra-virgin olive oil, divided
  1 cup chopped onion
  1 red bell pepper, cut into ⅓-inch dice
4½ teaspoons fresh thyme leaves, divided
  2 garlic cloves, minced
  4 ounces haricots verts or slender green beans, trimmed, cut into ¾-inch pieces
     (about 1 cup)
  2 small zucchini, trimmed, cut into ⅓-inch dice
  1 cup fresh corn kernels (cut from 2 ears of corn)

  4 skinless boneless chicken breast halves
  4 thin slices country ham or prosciutto (each about 6x3 inches)
  ½ cup all purpose flour

  2 tablespoons whipping cream

Heat 1 tablespoon oil in large nonstick skillet over medium-high heat. Add onion; sauté until beginning to soften, 3 minutes. Add bell pepper, 1½ teaspoons thyme, and garlic; sauté 1 minute. Add beans; sauté until just beginning to soften, about 3 minutes. Add zucchini; sauté until all vegetables are crisp-tender, 4 minutes longer. Stir in corn; remove from heat.

Cover cutting board with large sheet of plastic wrap. Arrange chicken, smooth side up, on plastic wrap, spacing several inches apart. Sprinkle with remaining 3 teaspoons thyme, then pepper. Place 1 ham slice on each chicken breast, trimming so edges extend slightly over chicken. Place another sheet of plastic wrap atop chicken breasts. Using meat mallet or rolling pin, pound evenly to scant ½-inch thickness. Turn chicken over and sprinkle lightly with salt and pepper, then flour.

Heat 2 tablespoons oil in each of 2 heavy large skillets over medium-high heat. Divide chicken between skillets, ham side up, and cook until edges of chicken begin to turn opaque, about 4 minutes.

Turn chicken over and cook until cooked through, 4 minutes longer. Remove from heat; cover.

Rewarm succotash over medium-high heat, stirring constantly. Mix in cream; season with salt and pepper.

Transfer chicken to plates, ham side up. Spoon succotash alongside.

4 SERVINGS

Spicy Chipotle Grilled Chicken

¼ cup canned chipotle chiles in adobo*

3 tablespoons olive oil

2 garlic cloves, pressed

½ onion, coarsely chopped

2 tablespoons chopped fresh cilantro

1 tablespoon paprika

1 teaspoon ground cumin

1 teaspoon chili powder

1 teaspoon salt

1 3½-pound chicken, cut into 8 pieces

Nonstick vegetable oil spray

There's depth, subtlety, and just the right amount of heat here. Start preparing this dish one day ahead since the chicken needs to marinate overnight.

Combine chipotles in adobo, olive oil, and garlic cloves in processor; puree until paste forms. Add chopped onion, chopped cilantro, paprika, ground cumin, chili powder, and salt; process until onion is finely chopped. Transfer ¼ cup chipotle mixture to small bowl; cover and refrigerate. Arrange chicken pieces in 11x7x2-inch glass baking dish. Spread remaining chipotle mixture all over chicken pieces. Cover and refrigerate overnight.

Spray grill rack with nonstick spray. Prepare barbecue (medium heat). Grill chicken until cooked through, moving to cooler part of grill as needed to prevent burning and brushing with reserved marinade during last 5 minutes of grilling, about 30 minutes. Transfer chicken to platter and serve.

Canned chipotle chiles in adobo are available at some supermarkets and at Latin markets nationwide.

4 SERVINGS

Chicken, Asparagus, and Broccoli Stir-Fry

    2   tablespoons Asian sesame oil, divided
    2   garlic cloves, chopped
    2   cups 1½-inch pieces asparagus
    2   cups small broccoli florets
    6   tablespoons low-salt chicken broth, divided

  1¼   pounds skinless boneless chicken breast halves, thinly sliced crosswise
    4   large green onions, chopped
    3   tablespoons hoisin sauce*
    1   tablespoon oyster sauce*

Heat 1 tablespoon oil in large nonstick skillet over medium-high heat. Add garlic and stir 30 seconds. Stir in asparagus pieces and broccoli florets; add 4 tablespoons broth. Cover and cook until vegetables are crisp-tender, about 3 minutes. Transfer vegetables to bowl.

Add remaining 1 tablespoon oil to skillet. Sprinkle chicken with salt and pepper; add chicken and green onions to skillet. Stir-fry until chicken is just cooked through, about 3 minutes. Mix in hoisin sauce, oyster sauce, vegetables, and remaining 2 tablespoons broth. Toss until heated through and evenly coated with sauce, about 1 minute. Season to taste with salt and pepper and serve.

Available in the Asian foods section of many supermarkets and at Asian markets.

4 SERVINGS

Tamarind-Glazed Turkey Burgers

GLAZE

2 tablespoons canola oil

1 tablespoon minced peeled fresh ginger

½ cup tamarind concentrate*

½ cup honey

¼ cup water

2 tablespoons fresh lime juice

BURGERS

½ cup mayonnaise

1 tablespoon minced peeled fresh ginger

2 teaspoons salt

1 red jalapeño chile with seeds, minced

1 teaspoon ground black pepper

½ cup chopped green onions

2½ pounds ground natural turkey

8 4-inch-diameter rolls (such as potato or kaiser), split horizontally

Add sliced red onion and tomato as well as lettuce to make these burgers complete.

FOR GLAZE: Heat oil in heavy medium saucepan over medium-high heat. Add ginger and sauté 2 minutes. Add tamarind concentrate, honey, and water and bring to boil. Reduce heat; simmer until thick enough to coat spoon and reduced to 1¼ cups, stirring often, about 8 minutes. Cool completely (volume will reduce as glaze cools); mix in lime juice. (*Can be made 2 days ahead. Cover and chill.*)

FOR BURGERS: Stir mayonnaise, ginger, salt, jalapeño, pepper, and 4 teaspoons glaze in large bowl to blend; mix in onions. Add turkey; blend gently (do not pack tightly). Shape mixture into eight ½-inch-thick patties. Arrange on small baking sheet. (*Can be made 8 hours ahead. Cover and chill.*)

Prepare barbecue (medium heat). Grill rolls, cut side down, until golden, about 2 minutes; transfer to work surface. Grill burgers until cooked through and thermometer inserted into center registers 160°F, about 8 minutes per side. Brush each burger with glaze. Place 1 burger, glazed side down, on each roll bottom; brush each burger with more glaze. Serve, passing remaining glaze separately.

Sometimes labeled tamarind paste, tamarind concentrate is a dark, seedless paste with a tart-sweet flavor. It's available at Middle Eastern and Indian markets, and at some Asian markets.

MAKES 8

Seared Duck Breasts with Red-Wine Sauce and Candied Kumquats

2¼ cups fruity red wine, such as Beaujolais
¾ cup chopped shallots (about 3 large)
4½ tablespoons balsamic vinegar
22 whole black peppercorns, crushed
12 coriander seeds, crushed
1 cup plus 2 tablespoons fresh orange juice
3 cups low-salt chicken broth

3 1-pound Muscovy duck breast halves with skin

Candied Kumquats (see recipe)

Additional crushed whole black peppercorns

Combine first 5 ingredients in medium saucepan. Boil until reduced to 1½ cups, about 12 minutes. Add orange juice and boil 5 minutes. Add chicken broth and boil until reduced to 3 cups, about 15 minutes. Strain. (*Sauce can be made 2 days ahead. Cover and chill.*)

Preheat oven to 250°F. Using sharp knife, score skin of duck breasts diagonally to create ¾-inch-wide diamond pattern. Sprinkle duck with salt and pepper. Heat 1 large and 1 medium skillet over medium-high heat. Place 2 duck breasts, skin side down, in large skillet and remaining breast in medium skillet. Cook until skin is crisp, about 8 minutes. Turn; cook until brown and thermometer inserted into center registers 130°F for medium-rare, about 6 minutes. Transfer to rimmed baking sheet and place in oven to keep warm.

Drain kumquats, reserving syrup. Pour off fat from skillets, reserving 2 tablespoons fat in large skillet for sauce. Heat large skillet with fat over medium-high heat. Add reserved sauce and 4½ tablespoons reserved kumquat syrup. Boil until sauce is thickened and reduced to ¾ cup, about 5 minutes.

Slice duck breasts crosswise into ½-inch-thick slices. Divide duck breast slices among 6 plates. Drizzle duck with red wine sauce, garnish with Candied Kumquats, sprinkle with crushed peppercorns, and serve.

6 SERVINGS

Candied Kumquats

1 cup water
½ cup sugar
4 ounces kumquats (about 14), each cut crosswise into 4 slices, seeded

Bring water and sugar to boil in heavy small saucepan, stirring until sugar dissolves. Add kumquat slices. Reduce heat to medium and simmer until kumquats become translucent and tender, stirring occasionally, about 15 minutes. Cool. *(Candied Kumquats can be made 3 days ahead. Cover and chill.)*

MAKES ABOUT ½ CUP

An update of duck à l'orange, this recipe replaces whole duck with Muscovy duck breasts, and the syrupy orange glaze of yore with a red-wine sauce and tart-sweet candied kumquats. It is lovely with celery root puree and an Oregon Pinto Noir.

Seared Wild Salmon with New Potatoes and Dijon Broth

<table>
<tr><td>1½</td><td>pounds new or baby red-skinned potatoes, unpeeled</td></tr>
<tr><td>2</td><td>tablespoons butter</td></tr>
<tr><td>2</td><td>tablespoons canola oil</td></tr>
<tr><td>4</td><td>6- to 8-ounce skinless wild salmon fillets</td></tr>
<tr><td>2</td><td>cups dry white wine</td></tr>
<tr><td>2</td><td>large shallots, thinly sliced</td></tr>
<tr><td>2</td><td>tablespoons apple cider vinegar</td></tr>
<tr><td>1½</td><td>cups low-salt chicken broth</td></tr>
<tr><td>2</td><td>tablespoons chopped fresh tarragon leaves plus sprigs for garnish</td></tr>
<tr><td>1</td><td>tablespoon Dijon mustard</td></tr>
<tr><td>2</td><td>tablespoons olive oil</td></tr>
<tr><td>1½</td><td>pounds baby spinach leaves, divided</td></tr>
</table>

Preheat oven to 400°F. Place potatoes in large saucepan and cover with cold water by 1 inch. Bring to boil; reduce heat to medium-high and boil until almost cooked through, about 12 minutes. Drain; cool. Cut potatoes in half.

Melt 2 tablespoons butter with canola oil in heavy large skillet over high heat. Season salmon fillets with salt and pepper. Place salmon, flat side up, in skillet. Cook until brown, about 4 minutes. Turn salmon over and cook 2 minutes. Carefully arrange salmon, flat side down, in large baking dish. Scatter potatoes around salmon.

Combine wine, shallots, and vinegar in heavy large saucepan. Boil until reduced to 1 cup, about 7 minutes. Add chicken broth, chopped tarragon, and mustard. Bring just to boil. Pour hot broth over salmon and potatoes in dish. Bake until salmon and potatoes are cooked through, about 20 minutes.

About 5 minutes before salmon is done cooking, heat olive oil in heavy large pot. Add half of spinach to pot; stir until wilted, about 3 minutes. Add remaining spinach and toss just until wilted.

Divide spinach among 4 shallow bowls. Top with salmon fillets. Divide potatoes and broth among bowls; garnish with tarragon sprigs.

4 SERVINGS

Ask your fishmonger to skin the salmon fillets for you.

Oil-Poached Tuna with Escarole and Lima Beans

1   lemon, thinly sliced
1   10-ounce albacore tuna fillet, cut into 1/3-inch-thick slices
    Olive oil (for poaching)

1   large green onion, thinly sliced (about 1/4 cup)
4   cups coarsely chopped escarole (about 4 ounces)
1   8 1/2-ounce can baby lima beans, drained
4   tablespoons chopped fresh parsley, divided
1   tablespoon white balsamic vinegar

Line heavy medium skillet with lemon slices. Sprinkle tuna with salt and pepper and place atop lemon. Add just enough olive oil to cover tuna. Poach tuna over medium-low heat until almost cooked through, about 3 minutes. Using slotted spoon, transfer tuna to plate. Discard lemon slices.

Discard all but 1 tablespoon drippings from skillet. Add green onion and sauté over medium-high heat 1 minute. Add escarole, lima beans, and 3 tablespoons parsley to skillet. Sauté until escarole begins to wilt, about 1 minute. Sprinkle with vinegar. Season to taste with salt and pepper.

Divide escarole-bean mixture between 2 plates and top with tuna slices. Sprinkle with remaining 1 tablespoon parsley and serve.

2 SERVINGS

Poaching fish in olive oil—a popular restaurant technique—is surprisingly easy and well suited to every-night cooking.

Crispy Skate with Cauliflower, Bacon, Capers, and Croutons

CAULIFLOWER

    4 slices thick-cut bacon, cut into 1-inch pieces
    2 cups small (¾-inch) cauliflower florets
   10 cherry tomatoes, halved
 1½ tablespoons fresh lemon juice
    1 tablespoon drained capers
  ¼ teaspoon chopped fresh thyme

SKATE

  ¼ cup rice flour*
  ¼ cup Cream of Wheat
  ¼ teaspoon chopped fresh tarragon
  ¼ teaspoon chopped fresh thyme
    2 7-ounce pieces boned skate wing (or Dover sole fillets)
  ¼ cup canola oil

    2 tablespoons coarsely chopped purchased plain croutons

FOR CAULIFLOWER: Sauté bacon in heavy large skillet over medium heat until brown and crisp. Using slotted spoon, transfer bacon to paper towels to drain. Add cauliflower to drippings in skillet and sauté until crisp-tender and beginning to brown, about 5 minutes. Add tomatoes, lemon juice, capers, and thyme; simmer 1 minute. Remove from heat.

FOR SKATE: Whisk rice flour, Cream of Wheat, and herbs in large shallow bowl to blend. Sprinkle fish with salt and pepper. Coat fish on both sides with flour mixture. Heat oil in another heavy large skillet over medium-high heat. Add fish. Sauté until brown and just opaque in center, about 3 minutes per side.

Rewarm cauliflower mixture over medium heat. Mix in bacon and croutons. Season to taste with salt and pepper. Spoon cauliflower mixture into center of 2 plates; top with fish.

Available at some supermarkets, specialty foods stores, and natural foods stores.

2 SERVINGS

Salmon with Beurre Rouge and Smoked-Salmon-Stuffed Baked Potato

½ cup dry red wine
¼ cup minced shallots
½ teaspoon red wine vinegar

2 8-ounce Yukon Gold potatoes
  Fine sea salt
10 tablespoons (1¼ sticks) chilled unsalted butter, divided
2 tablespoons whole milk
½ cup sour cream
4 tablespoons chopped green onion tops, divided

4 ounces smoked salmon, chopped

¼ cup water
4 7- to 8-ounce skinless salmon fillets, each cut lengthwise into 2 strips

  Cracked black peppercorns
  Chopped fresh chives

Bring wine, shallots, and vinegar to boil in heavy small saucepan. Reduce heat to low and simmer until liquid is reduced to 2 tablespoons, about 5 minutes. Remove pan from heat and cover. (*Can be made 4 hours ahead. Let stand at room temperature.*)

Preheat oven to 400°F. Place each potato on separate sheet of foil, sprinkle with sea salt, and wrap tightly. Bake until tender, about 1 hour. Remove foil; cool to just warm, about 20 minutes. Cut lengthwise in half. Scoop flesh into microwave-safe bowl, leaving ¼-inch-thick potato shell. Add 2 tablespoons butter and milk to potatoes in bowl; mash well. Stir in sour cream and 3 tablespoons green onion tops. Season to taste with salt and pepper. (*Can be made 2 hours ahead. Loosely cover shells and filling separately and let each stand at room temperature.*)

Rewarm potato shells, then filling, in microwave at 20-second intervals until heated through. Stir smoked salmon into filling; season with sea salt and pepper. Mound filling in shells.

Place ¼ cup water and salmon fillets in heavy large skillet; sprinkle with salt and pepper. Cover; steam over medium-high heat until salmon is just opaque in center, about 3 minutes.

Meanwhile, rewarm wine-shallot reduction over medium-low heat. Add remaining 8 tablespoons butter, 1 tablespoon at a time, whisking until each is melted before adding next; continue whisking until beurre rouge is thick (do not overheat or sauce may separate). Season with salt and pepper.

Spoon sauce onto 4 plates. Place potatoes on 1 side; sprinkle with remaining green onions. Arrange 2 salmon strips atop sauce on each plate; sprinkle with peppercorns and chives.

4 SERVINGS

Beurre rouge, the red wine version of the classic butter sauce beurre blanc, works well with salmon: The sauce's tartness plays off the salmon's silky richness. Uncork a Pinot Noir.

Roasted Halibut and Green Beans with Cilantro Sauce

    2 cups loosely packed cilantro leaves (from 1 large bunch)
    2 tablespoons fresh lemon juice
    1 green onion, chopped (about ¼ cup)
    1 tablespoon minced peeled fresh ginger
    ½ jalapeño chile with seeds, chopped (about 2 teaspoons)
    5 tablespoons safflower oil, divided
    2 teaspoons Asian sesame oil, divided
    3 teaspoons soy sauce, divided

    2 8-ounce halibut fillets, each about 1 inch thick
    2 cups green beans
    2 cups oyster mushrooms or stemmed shiitake mushrooms

Preheat oven to 450°F. Place first 5 ingredients, 3 tablespoons safflower oil, 1 teaspoon sesame oil, and 1 teaspoon soy sauce in processor; puree. Season with salt.

Place fish fillets, beans, and mushrooms in single layer on rimmed baking sheet. Whisk 2 tablespoons safflower oil, 1 teaspoon sesame oil, and 2 teaspoons soy sauce in bowl to blend. Pour over fish, beans, and mushrooms; toss vegetables to coat. Sprinkle with salt and pepper. Roast until fish is opaque in center and beans are crisp-tender, about 8 minutes. Divide fish, vegetables, and sauce between plates.

2 SERVINGS

Whole Branzino Roasted in Salt

FISH

- 1 3-pound box coarse kosher salt
- 5 (or more) large egg whites
- 2 1- to 1½-pound whole branzino, loup de mer, or sea bass, gutted
- 8 fresh parsley sprigs
- 2 fresh thyme sprigs
- 4 thin lemon slices

SALSA VERDE

- 1 lemon
- ¼ cup finely diced celery
- ¼ cup finely diced cucumber
- ¼ cup finely chopped fresh parsley
- ¼ cup extra-virgin olive oil
- 2 tablespoons drained small capers
- 2 tablespoons sliced pitted brine-cured green olives (such as picholine)
- 3 cups arugula

FOR FISH: Preheat oven to 400°F. Stir salt and 5 egg whites in large bowl, adding more egg whites as needed to form grainy paste. Press ¼-inch layer of salt mixture (large enough to hold both fish) onto large rimmed baking sheet. Stuff cavity of each whole fish with half of herb sprigs and lemon slices. Place fish atop salt mixture on baking sheet. Pack remaining salt mixture over fish to enclose completely. Roast until thermometer inserted into thickest part of fish registers 135°F, about 20 minutes. Let stand 10 minutes.

MEANWHILE, PREPARE SALSA VERDE: Using small sharp knife, remove peel and white pith from lemon. Working over bowl, cut between membranes to release segments. Cut each segment into 3 pieces. Add lemon pieces and next 6 ingredients to bowl.

Using back of large spoon, gently crack open salt crust on fish. Lift and discard salt layer. Pull skin from top of 1 fish. Carefully lift top fillet from bones and transfer to plate. Lift and discard bones. Gently lift second fillet from skin and transfer to second plate. Repeat with second fish for a total of 4 plates.

Spoon salsa verde over fish, leaving juices in bowl. Add arugula to bowl; toss to coat. Divide among plates.

4 SERVINGS

The French call it *loup de mer* and the Italians call it *branzino*, but it's the same fish—Mediterranean sea bass. Roasting the fish in salt makes it very moist—without, surprisingly, making it taste too salty. The lemony salsa verde adds zing and freshness that contrast nicely with the roasted fish.

Grilled Tilapia with Béarnaise Sabayon

  1 cup dry white wine
½ cup minced shallots
  2 fresh tarragon sprigs
  1 teaspoon white wine vinegar

¾ cup plus 3 tablespoons water
  8 baby bok choy, trimmed, cut lengthwise in half through core
    Fine sea salt

  4 large egg yolks
  2 tablespoons chopped fresh tarragon

  4 7- to 8-ounce tilapia fillets
  2 tablespoons canola oil

Boil first 4 ingredients in heavy small saucepan until liquid is reduced to 2 tablespoons, about 9 minutes. Cover and remove from heat. Remove tarragon sprigs and discard. (*Can be made 4 hours ahead. Let stand at room temperature.*)

Prepare barbecue (medium-high heat). Combine ¾ cup water and bok choy in large pot. Cover and cook over high heat until crisp-tender, turning occasionally, about 5 minutes. Drain. Sprinkle bok choy with sea salt and pepper. Cover to keep warm.

Whisk egg yolks and 3 tablespoons water in medium metal bowl. Set bowl over saucepan of barely simmering water. Whisk until mixture is light and foamy and thermometer inserted into center registers 160°F, about 2 minutes. Whisk in shallot-wine reduction and chopped tarragon. Season sabayon with salt and pepper. Remove from heat.

Immediately sprinkle fish with sea salt and pepper; brush with canola oil. Grill until slightly charred and just opaque in center, about 3 minutes per side.

Divide bok choy among 4 plates. Place tilapia alongside bok choy. Spoon warm béarnaise sabayon over fish.

4 SERVINGS

Grilled Halibut, Eggplant, and Baby Bok Choy with Korean Barbecue Sauce

  4 tablespoons olive oil or vegetable oil, divided
  2 garlic cloves, minced
1½ teaspoons minced serrano chile with seeds
⅓ cup soy sauce
¼ cup (packed) dark brown sugar

Asian Dinner for 4

Sushi Platter

Grilled Halibut, Eggplant, and
Baby Bok Choy with
Korean Barbecue Sauce
(opposite; pictured at left)

Steamed White Rice

Riesling

Chai-Spiced Almond Cookies
(page 228)

Sliced Mango

Tea

3 tablespoons unseasoned rice vinegar
3 tablespoons water
1 tablespoon Asian sesame oil

8 baby bok choy, halved lengthwise
4 medium-size Japanese eggplants, trimmed, halved lengthwise
4 6- to 7-ounce halibut fillets (each about 1 inch thick)
2 green onions, thinly sliced

Heat 1 tablespoon olive oil in heavy small saucepan over medium heat. Add garlic and chile; sauté until fragrant and light golden, about 3 minutes. Add soy sauce, brown sugar, vinegar, and 3 tablespoons water and bring to boil, stirring until sugar dissolves. Reduce heat to medium and simmer until mixture is reduced to 3/4 cup, about 5 minutes (sauce will be thin). Remove barbecue sauce from heat; whisk in sesame oil. Transfer 1/4 cup barbecue sauce to small bowl and reserve.

Prepare barbecue (medium heat). Combine bok choy and eggplant halves in large bowl. Drizzle 2 tablespoons olive oil over and toss to coat. Sprinkle with salt and pepper. Brush fish with remaining 1 tablespoon olive oil; sprinkle with salt and pepper. Grill vegetables and fish until vegetables are tender and slightly charred and fish is just opaque in center, turning occasionally and brushing with sauce, about 10 minutes total for vegetables and 7 minutes total for fish. Transfer vegetables and fish to plates; sprinkle with green onions. Drizzle with reserved sauce and serve.

4 SERVINGS

Sautéed Cod with Garlic-Herb Vinaigrette and Baked Portobello Mushrooms

VINAIGRETTE

1	whole head of garlic
1½	tablespoons Sherry wine vinegar
1½	teaspoons Dijon mustard
1½	teaspoons chopped fresh chives
1½	teaspoons chopped Italian parsley
1	teaspoon minced shallot
1	teaspoon chopped fresh tarragon
½	cup extra-virgin olive oil
	Fine sea salt

MUSHROOMS

4	4- to 5-inch-diameter portobello mushrooms, stemmed
⅓	cup extra-virgin olive oil
2	garlic cloves, chopped
8	fresh rosemary sprigs
8	fresh thyme sprigs

FISH

4	7- to 8-ounce skinless cod fillets
	Quick-cooking flour (such as Wondra)
2	tablespoons canola oil

FOR VINAIGRETTE: Preheat oven to 400°F. Wrap garlic in foil. Place foil packet directly on oven rack and roast garlic until tender, about 40 minutes. Cool garlic. Peel and finely mash enough garlic to measure 1 tablespoon packed. Place mashed garlic in heavy small saucepan. Add vinegar and next 5 ingredients. Gradually whisk in olive oil. Season with sea salt and pepper. (*Vinaigrette can be made 1 day ahead. Cover and refrigerate.*)

FOR MUSHROOMS: Preheat oven to 400°F. Brush mushrooms all over with olive oil. Place mushrooms, rounded side down, on foil-lined baking sheet. Sprinkle with sea salt and pepper, then chopped garlic. Arrange 2 rosemary sprigs and 2 thyme sprigs on each. Roast mushrooms until tender, about 25 minutes.

MEANWHILE, PREPARE FISH: Sprinkle fish with sea salt and pepper; dust lightly with flour. Heat canola oil in heavy large skillet over medium-high heat. Add fish and sauté until brown and just opaque in center, about 5 minutes per side.

Whisk vinaigrette over low heat to warm slightly. Thinly slice each mushroom on slight diagonal; overlap slices in row on 1 side of each plate. Spoon vinaigrette onto opposite side of plate; top with fish.

4 SERVINGS

Chile-Glazed Halibut with Avocado-Tomatillo Sauce

GLAZE

- 6 tablespoons fresh orange juice
- 6 tablespoons honey
- 1½ teaspoons minced canned chipotle chiles
- 1 garlic clove, coarsely chopped
- ¼ teaspoon ground cinnamon

SAUCE

- 1 large avocado, halved, pitted, peeled
- 2 medium tomatillos (about 4 ounces), husked, rinsed, coarsely chopped
- ¼ cup fresh orange juice
- ¼ teaspoon (or more) hot pepper sauce

FISH

- 6 5-ounce halibut fillets (each about 1 inch thick)
- 1 orange with skin, cut lengthwise in half, thinly sliced crosswise
  Ground cumin

FOR GLAZE: Mix all ingredients in blender until smooth. Season with salt and pepper. (*Can be prepared 1 day ahead. Cover and refrigerate. Stir before using.*)

FOR SAUCE: Combine all ingredients in blender; blend until smooth. (*Can be made 2 hours ahead. Cover; let stand at room temperature.*)

FOR FISH: Prepare barbecue (medium heat). Make crosswise slits in each fillet, cutting to within ¼ inch of bottom and spacing slits about ¾ inch apart. Brush glaze over top and into slits. Place orange slices in slits. Sprinkle fish with ground cumin, salt, and pepper. Place fish, orange side up, on grill; cover and cook until fish is opaque, about 8 minutes. Using wide spatula, carefully transfer fish to platter. Let rest several minutes. Spoon avocado sauce onto plates, spreading slightly. Arrange 1 fillet over sauce on each plate and serve.

6 SERVINGS

Southwestern Supper for 6

Guacamole, Salsa, and
Tortilla Chips

Chile-Glazed Halibut with
Avocado-Tomatillo Sauce
(*at left*)

Black Beans

White Rice

Sauvignon Blanc

Warm Baby Bananas with
Dulce de Leche Sauce
(*page 183*)

Baked Cod and Potatoes
with Mustard-Horseradish Sauce

Nonstick vegetable oil spray

½ cup mayonnaise

3 tablespoons Dijon mustard with horseradish

2 tablespoons fresh lemon juice

⅔ pound unpeeled red-skinned potatoes, thinly sliced

2 6-ounce cod fillets

2 tablespoons chopped fresh parsley

Preheat oven to 400°F. Line rimmed baking sheet with foil; coat with nonstick spray. Mix mayonnaise, mustard, and lemon juice in medium bowl to blend. Season with pepper.

Toss potatoes in mustard mixture. Gently shake excess mixture from potatoes before spreading in single layer on ¾ of baking sheet. Bake until potatoes are beginning to brown, about 13 minutes. Coat fish with remaining mustard mixture. Sprinkle with salt and pepper. Place fish alongside potatoes. Bake until opaque in center and potatoes are tender, about 10 minutes longer.

Divide potatoes between 2 plates; sprinkle lightly with salt. Top potatoes with fish, sprinkle with chopped parsley, and serve.

2 SERVINGS

Spicy Salmon with Tomatoes and Star Anise

1 tablespoon Asian sesame oil

4 6-ounce wild salmon fillets with skin

1 cup chopped red onion

2 teaspoons minced peeled fresh ginger

¾ teaspoon freshly ground star anise

¼ to ½ teaspoon dried crushed red pepper

4 plum tomatoes, seeded, chopped

2 tablespoons soy sauce

1½ tablespoons sugar

Preheat oven to 325°F. Heat oil in large nonstick skillet over medium heat. Add salmon, skin side down; cook 2 minutes. Cover pan; cook salmon 2 minutes longer. Transfer salmon, skin side down, to baking sheet. Place in oven; cook until just opaque in center, about 8 minutes.

Meanwhile, heat same skillet over medium heat. Add onion and next 3 ingredients; sauté until onion is golden, about 5 minutes. Stir in tomatoes, soy sauce, and sugar.

Increase heat to medium-high and cook mixture until slightly thickened, stirring occasionally, about 3 minutes. Divide salmon among 4 plates and top with tomato sauce.

4 SERVINGS

Lobster with Lemon-Herb Butter

6 1¼- to 1½-pound live lobsters

1 cup (2 sticks) butter
2 teaspoons fresh lemon juice
2 teaspoons chopped fresh Italian parsley
2 teaspoons chopped fresh chives
2 teaspoons chopped fresh basil

Lemon wedges

Cook lobsters in 2 large pots of boiling salted water until shells are pink and lobsters are just cooked through, about 11 minutes.

Meanwhile, melt butter in small saucepan. Add lemon juice and herbs. Season with salt and pepper.

Serve lobsters with lemon wedges and warm herb butter.

6 SERVINGS

Coleslaw, a great loaf of bread, and a bottle of Chablis are all you need with this.

Sautéed Scallops with Cherry Tomatoes, Green Onions, and Parsley

1½	pounds large sea scallops, side muscles removed
	Fleur de sel or coarse kosher salt
4	tablespoons extra-virgin olive oil, divided
4	large green onions, chopped, white and green parts separated
1	12-ounce container cherry tomatoes or grape tomatoes
4	tablespoons coarsely chopped fresh Italian parsley, divided
3	tablespoons fresh lemon juice
½	teaspoon mild Spanish paprika (pimentón dulce) or Hungarian sweet paprika

Rinse and drain scallops; pat dry with paper towels. Sprinkle with fleur de sel and pepper. Heat 2 tablespoons oil in large skillet over medium-high heat. Add scallops; sauté until browned outside and just opaque in center, about 2 minutes per side. Transfer scallops to plate; cover. Add 1 tablespoon oil to same skillet; add white parts of green onions and sauté until almost tender, about 1 minute. Add tomatoes and green parts of onions and sauté until tomatoes begin to burst and release juices, about 5 minutes. Stir in 3 tablespoons parsley, lemon juice, and paprika. Return scallops and any accumulated juices to skillet and stir just until heated through, about 1 minute. Season with salt and pepper. Transfer scallop mixture to platter. Drizzle with 1 tablespoon oil and sprinkle with 1 tablespoon chopped fresh parsley.

4 SERVINGS

Spiny Lobster in "Crazy Water"

2	1½- to 1¾-pound wild-caught spiny lobsters or Maine lobsters
¾	cup extra-virgin olive oil, divided
6	garlic cloves, thinly sliced
	Pinch of dried crushed red pepper
2	12-ounce containers cherry tomatoes (about 4½ cups)
1	cup dry white wine
¾	cup water
2	tablespoons chopped fresh Italian parsley

"Crazy Water," or *acqua pazza*, is actually a fisherman's recipe from the Campania region of Italy; the sauce is traditionally made with garlic, parsley, white wine, and tomato (and seawater, if you happen to have some on hand).

Preheat oven to 325°F. Cook lobsters in large covered pot of boiling salted water 3 minutes (lobsters will not be fully cooked). Using tongs, transfer lobsters to large rimmed baking sheet. Let stand until lobsters are cool enough to handle, about 20 minutes. Using kitchen shears or sharp knife, cut lobsters in half lengthwise. Rinse away any dark parts from body cavity. Pat dry. Sprinkle with salt and pepper.

Heat ¼ cup oil in each of 2 large ovenproof skillets over medium heat. Add 2 lobster halves to each skillet, flesh side down, and cook until lightly golden, about 2 minutes. Divide garlic and crushed red pepper between skillets and sauté until garlic begins to brown, stirring occasionally, about 2 minutes. Divide tomatoes between skillets and cook until slightly wilted. Divide wine between skillets and cook 3 minutes. Divide water between skillets; turn lobsters flesh side up, cover, and braise in oven until lobsters are cooked through, about 5 minutes.

Transfer lobsters to 2 plates. Combine tomato mixtures in 1 skillet. Boil sauce until reduced to 3 cups, about 5 minutes. Season with salt and pepper. Stir in parsley. Pour sauce over lobsters. Drizzle 2 tablespoons oil over each lobster and serve.

2 SERVINGS

Shrimp and Peppers with Spicy Rice

  2 tablespoons extra-virgin olive oil
  2 teaspoons plus 1 tablespoon balsamic vinegar
  4 green onions, chopped, divided

  1 pound uncooked medium shrimp, peeled, deveined
  1 tablespoon fresh lime juice
2½ cups bottled clam juice
 ½ teaspoon annatto powder*

 ¼ cup olive oil
  1 cup chopped onion
 ½ green bell pepper, seeded, chopped
  1 garlic clove, chopped
  2 plum tomatoes, seeded, chopped
  2 tablespoons chopped fresh cilantro
 ½ to 1 whole Scotch bonnet chile or habanero chile, seeded, chopped
  1 cup medium-grain white rice

Whisk extra-virgin olive oil, 2 teaspoons vinegar, and 2 chopped green onions in small bowl. Season dressing with salt and pepper.

Toss shrimp with lime juice in bowl. Let stand 30 minutes. Bring clam juice and annatto powder to boil in small saucepan, stirring to dissolve. Cover and set aside.

Heat ¼ cup olive oil in heavy large skillet over medium-high heat. Add shrimp with any juices to pan; sprinkle with salt and sauté until just opaque in center, about 3 minutes. Transfer to plate. Add onion, green pepper, and garlic to pan; sauté 2 minutes. Add tomatoes, cilantro, chile, and 1 chopped green onion to pan. Reduce heat to medium and sauté until vegetables are almost tender, about 3 minutes. Add 1 tablespoon vinegar and rice; stir 2 minutes. Add clam juice mixture. Boil rice mixture 1 minute. Reduce heat to low, cover, and cook until rice is tender and broth is absorbed, about 20 minutes. Season with salt and pepper. Stir in shrimp. Cover and cook until shrimp are heated through, about 1 minute. Transfer to bowl. Sprinkle with 1 chopped green onion. Serve with dressing.

Available in the spice section of some supermarkets and at Latin markets.

4 SERVINGS

Jumbo Shrimp with Chive Butter

¼ cup Dijon mustard
¼ cup fresh lemon juice
1 cup (2 sticks) butter, melted
6 tablespoons chopped fresh chives

36 uncooked jumbo shrimp, peeled, deveined, butterflied
Whole chives

The chive butter is a breeze to make, and it works overtime: First it's used to baste the shrimp, later it becomes the sauce.

Preheat broiler. Place mustard in bowl; whisk in lemon juice, then melted butter. Add chopped chives. Season with pepper.

Arrange shrimp, cut side up, on broiler pan. Brush with some of butter mixture. Broil until just cooked through, about 4 minutes. Arrange on plates and garnish with whole chives. Serve, passing remaining butter separately.

6 SERVINGS

Pan-Seared Sea Scallops with Lentils, Bacon, and Cider Reduction

MASCARPONE CREAM

- ½ cup dry white wine
- 2 tablespoons chopped shallots
- ¼ cup whipping cream
- ¼ cup mascarpone cheese
- 1 teaspoon finely grated lemon peel
- ½ teaspoon chopped fresh chives

CIDER REDUCTION

- 2 cups apple cider
- 1 cup apple cider vinegar
- ¼ cup chopped shallots

LENTILS

- 6 whole cloves
- 1 medium onion, peeled
- 6 cups water
- 1½ cups French green lentils (lentilles du Puy; about 12 ounces)
- 2 bay leaves
- 6 slices thick-cut applewood-smoked bacon, cut crosswise ¼ inch thick
- ¼ cup chopped shallots
- 1 teaspoon chopped fresh thyme

SCALLOPS

- 6 tablespoons butter, divided
- 18 sea scallops, patted dry
- 2 tablespoons olive oil

  Fresh thyme sprigs

FOR MASCARPONE CREAM: Place wine and shallots in heavy small saucepan. Boil until almost dry, about 6 minutes. Add cream. Boil until reduced by half, about 2 minutes. Stir in mascarpone, lemon peel, and chives. (*Can be made 1 day ahead. Transfer to small bowl; cover and chill. Rewarm before serving.*)

FOR CIDER REDUCTION: Place cider, vinegar, and shallots in heavy medium saucepan. Boil until reduced to ¾ cup, about 15 minutes. Strain; discard solids in strainer. Return cider mixture to pan. (*Cider reduction can be made 1 day ahead. Cover and refrigerate.*)

FOR LENTILS: Press thin end of cloves into peeled onion. Place onion in heavy large saucepan. Add 6 cups water, lentils, and bay leaves. Bring to boil. Reduce heat to medium-low and simmer until lentils are tender, stirring occasionally, about 30 minutes.

Meanwhile, cook bacon in heavy large skillet over medium heat until crisp. Using slotted spoon, transfer bacon to paper towels. Pour all but 3 tablespoons fat from skillet. Add shallots to skillet and sauté over medium heat until golden, about 2 minutes.

Drain lentils, discarding onion and bay leaves. Add bacon, lentils, and chopped thyme to shallots. (*Lentils can be made 2 hours ahead. Let stand at room temperature. Rewarm over medium heat, stirring often.*)

FOR SCALLOPS: Bring cider reduction to simmer. Whisk in 5 tablespoons butter, 1 tablespoon at a time. Keep warm.

Season scallops with salt and pepper. Melt 1 tablespoon butter with oil in heavy large skillet over medium-high heat. Add scallops and cook until brown, about 2 minutes per side.

Divide lentils among 6 plates. Arrange 3 scallops atop lentils on each plate. Drizzle cider reduction over scallops and around lentils. Drizzle warm mascarpone cream over. Garnish with thyme sprigs.

6 SERVINGS

Lentilles du Puy are lighter than other lentils and hold their shape especially well during cooking.

Lobster and Stone Crab Enchilado

2 uncooked frozen lobster tails (1½ pounds total), thawed, cut in half lengthwise, each half cut into thirds with shell intact
1 tablespoon fresh lime juice

¼ cup olive oil
⅓ cup chopped onion
2 tablespoons chopped green bell pepper
2 garlic cloves, chopped
1 tablespoon chopped fresh parsley
¼ teaspoon paprika
2 large plum tomatoes, seeded, diced
½ cup canned tomato puree
¾ cup bottled clam juice
½ cup dry Sherry wine
1 bay leaf
¼ teaspoon cayenne pepper
1 pound stone crab claws, cracked

A Cuban dish, *enchilado* (different from a Mexican enchilada) is seafood cooked in a mildly spicy tomato sauce. Serve this with rice, fried plantains, and a bottle of Viognier.

Place lobster and fresh lime juice in medium bowl; toss to coat. Let stand 15 minutes, tossing lobster occasionally.

Heat olive oil in heavy large pot over high heat. Add lobster pieces and any accumulated juices. Sauté until lobster shells turn bright orange, about 4 minutes. Using slotted spoon, return lobster to same bowl. Reduce heat to medium. Add chopped onion and chopped bell pepper to pot; sauté until soft, about 5 minutes. Add chopped garlic cloves, fresh parsley, and paprika and sauté 1 minute. Add diced tomatoes and tomato puree. Cook until juices thicken, stirring frequently, about 8 minutes. Add clam juice, Sherry, and bay leaf. Season to taste with salt. Add cayenne pepper. Bring mixture to boil, then add stone crab claws and reserved lobster with any accumulated juices. Reduce heat to medium-low, cover, and simmer until lobster meat is cooked through and tender, about 10 minutes.

2 SERVINGS

Mediterranean Supper Omelet with Fennel, Olives, and Dill

2 tablespoons olive oil, divided
2 cups thinly sliced fresh fennel bulb, fronds chopped and reserved
8 cherry tomatoes
¼ cup chopped pitted brine-cured green olives

5 large eggs, beaten to blend with ¼ teaspoon salt and ¼ teaspoon ground black pepper
½ 4-ounce package crumbled goat cheese Provençale (with thyme, basil, and sweet red pepper) or any herbed or peppered goat cheese
1½ tablespoons chopped fresh dill

Heat 1 tablespoon oil in 10-inch nonstick skillet over medium-high heat. Add fennel bulb; sauté until beginning to brown, about 5 minutes. Cover; cook until soft, stirring occasionally, about 4 minutes. Add tomatoes and mash with fork; mix in olives. Transfer to bowl.

Add 1 tablespoon oil to same skillet; heat over medium-high heat. Add eggs; cook until set in center, tilting skillet and lifting edges of omelet with spatula to let uncooked portion flow underneath, about 3 minutes. Sprinkle half of cheese over half of omelet; top with fennel mixture. Sprinkle dill over, then remaining cheese. Using spatula, fold uncovered half of omelet over cheese; slide onto plate. Garnish with fennel fronds.

2 SERVINGS

Winter Vegetables and Bulgur

2 tablespoons olive oil
4 cups ¾-inch pieces chopped peeled assorted root vegetables (such as carrots, turnips, celery root, and golden beets)
2 cups chopped onions
4 cups vegetable broth
1 rounded teaspoon herbes de Provence
1½ cups bulgur (about 8 ounces)
1 6-ounce package baby spinach leaves

MEATLESS

Heat oil in heavy large pot over high heat. Add root vegetables and onions; sauté until beginning to brown, about 10 minutes. Add vegetable broth and herbes de Provence; bring to boil. Add bulgur; cover pot and reduce heat to low. Simmer until bulgur is almost tender, stirring occasionally, about 15 minutes. Add spinach; stir until wilted, about 1 minute. Season to taste with salt and pepper.

4 SERVINGS

Asian Noodle Salad with Eggplant, Sugar Snap Peas, and Lime Dressing

    4 Japanese eggplants, unpeeled, cut on
       diagonal into ⅓-inch-thick slices
    8 ounces fresh shiitake mushrooms,
       stemmed
    2 bunches green onions, trimmed
    ¼ cup Asian sesame oil

    1 6-ounce package dried chuka soba*
       (Japanese-style) noodles
    1 8-ounce package sugar snap peas,
       trimmed

    7 tablespoons hoisin sauce*
   3½ tablespoons fresh lime juice
    4 teaspoons finely grated lime peel
   1½ tablespoons minced peeled fresh ginger

Prepare barbecue (medium-high heat). Combine first 3 ingredients; add sesame oil and toss to coat. Sprinkle with salt and pepper. Grill vegetables until tender, turning often, about 7 minutes for eggplant and mushrooms and 5 minutes for green onions. Transfer mushrooms and onions to cutting board; cool slightly. Slice mushrooms and onions.

Meanwhile, cook noodles in large pot of boiling salted water until almost tender but still firm to bite, about 3 minutes. Add sugar snap peas to noodles; cook 1 minute longer. Drain well. Transfer noodle mixture to large serving bowl. Add grilled vegetables.

Whisk last 4 ingredients in small bowl to blend. Toss noodle salad with dressing; season with salt and pepper.

Available in the Asian foods section of many supermarkets and at Asian markets.

4 SERVINGS

Black Bean Chili with Butternut Squash and Swiss Chard

    2 tablespoons olive oil
   2½ cups chopped onions
    3 garlic cloves, chopped
   2½ cups ½-inch pieces peeled butternut squash
    2 tablespoons chili powder
    2 teaspoons ground cumin
    3 15-ounce cans black beans, rinsed, drained

2½ cups vegetable broth
1 14½-ounce can diced tomatoes in juice
3 cups (packed) coarsely chopped Swiss chard leaves
    (from 1 small bunch)

Heat oil in heavy large pot over medium-high heat. Add onions and garlic; sauté until tender and golden, about 9 minutes. Add squash; stir 2 minutes. Stir in chili powder and cumin. Stir in beans, broth, and tomatoes with juices; bring to boil. Reduce heat and simmer, uncovered, until squash is tender, about 15 minutes. Stir in chard; simmer until chard is tender but still bright green, about 4 minutes longer. Season with salt and pepper. Ladle chili into bowls and serve.

4 SERVINGS

Top with chopped fresh cilantro, red onions, and grated cheddar cheese, if you like, and serve with ice-cold lager or lemonade.

Artichoke, Potato, and Portobello Mushroom Casserole

4 tablespoons extra-virgin olive oil, divided
1 lemon, halved
4 large artichokes
2 pounds Yukon Gold potatoes, thinly sliced
4 large portobello mushroom caps, thinly sliced
6 ounces soft fresh goat cheese
3 garlic cloves, minced
3 tablespoons freshly grated Parmesan cheese
½ cup dry white wine

Preheat oven to 425°F. Brush 13x9x2-inch glass baking dish with 1 tablespoon oil. Add juice from lemon half to large bowl of cold water. Cut off artichoke stems; rub cut surfaces with other lemon half. Peel off all leaves. Using spoon with serrated edge, scrape out fibrous choke from centers. Rub artichoke hearts all over with lemon. Slice hearts. Arrange half of potatoes in dish, covering bottom. Top with half of artichoke hearts and half of mushrooms. Coarsely crumble half of goat cheese over. Sprinkle with salt, pepper, and half of garlic, then 1 tablespoon Parmesan. Drizzle with 1 tablespoon oil. Cover with remaining mushrooms, then artichoke hearts, goat cheese, garlic, 1 tablespoon Parmesan, and 1 tablespoon oil. Top with remaining potatoes. Pour wine over; drizzle with 1 tablespoon oil. Cover with foil. Bake 40 minutes. Reduce oven temperature to 400°F. Sprinkle with 1 tablespoon Parmesan. Bake uncovered until potatoes are tender and top is brown, about 25 minutes.

8 SERVINGS

Quinoa with Moroccan Winter Squash and Carrot Stew

STEW

- 2 tablespoons olive oil
- 1 cup chopped onion
- 3 garlic cloves, chopped
- 2 teaspoons Hungarian sweet paprika
- 1 teaspoon salt
- ½ teaspoon ground black pepper
- ½ teaspoon ground coriander
- ½ teaspoon ground cumin
- ½ teaspoon turmeric
- ½ teaspoon ground ginger
- ½ teaspoon cayenne pepper
- Pinch of saffron
- 1 cup water
- 1 14½-ounce can diced tomatoes, drained
- 2 tablespoons fresh lemon juice
- 3 cups 1-inch cubes peeled butternut squash (from 1½-pound squash)
- 2 cups ¾-inch cubes peeled carrots

QUINOA

- 1 cup quinoa*
- 1 tablespoon butter
- 1 tablespoon olive oil
- ½ cup finely chopped onion
- ¼ cup finely chopped peeled carrot
- 2 garlic cloves, minced
- ½ teaspoon salt
- ½ teaspoon turmeric
- 2 cups water

- ½ cup chopped fresh cilantro, divided
- 2 teaspoons chopped fresh mint, divided

FOR STEW: Heat oil in large saucepan over medium heat. Add onion; sauté until soft, stirring often, about 5 minutes. Add garlic; stir 1 minute. Mix in paprika and next 8 ingredients. Add 1 cup water, tomatoes, and lemon juice. Bring to boil. Add squash and carrots. Cover; simmer over medium-low heat until vegetables are tender, stirring occasionally, about 20 minutes. Season with salt and pepper. (*Can be made 1 day ahead. Cover; chill.*)

FOR QUINOA: Rinse quinoa; drain. Melt butter with oil in large saucepan over medium heat. Add onion and carrot. Cover; cook until vegetables begin to brown, stirring often, about 10 minutes. Add garlic, salt, and turmeric; sauté 1 minute. Add quinoa; stir 1 minute. Add 2 cups water. Bring to boil; reduce heat to medium-low. Cover; simmer until liquid is absorbed and quinoa is tender, about 15 minutes.

Rewarm stew. Stir in half of cilantro and half of mint. Spoon quinoa onto platter, forming well in center. Spoon stew into well. Sprinkle remaining herbs over.

A grain with a delicate flavor and a texture similar to couscous; available at natural foods stores.

4 TO 6 SERVINGS

A gorgeous, satisfying vegetarian main course that's easy to make. Quinoa requires no pre-soaking, so it's as simple to do as rice. Partner the dish with a Pinot Noir.

Mushroom-Shallot Quiche

CRUST

1½ cups all purpose flour

1 teaspoon salt

1 teaspoon sugar

½ cup (1 stick) chilled unsalted butter, cut into ½-inch cubes

1 large egg

1 teaspoon cold water

1 large egg white, lightly beaten

FILLING

1½ tablespoons unsalted butter

⅓ cup chopped shallots (about 2 medium)

½ pound mushrooms, cut into ¼-inch slices

5 teaspoons chopped fresh thyme, divided

¾ cup whipping cream

2 large eggs

Pinch of salt

Pinch of ground black pepper

2 green onions (white and pale green parts only), thinly sliced

2 tablespoons finely grated Gruyère cheese

FOR CRUST: Blend flour, salt, and sugar in processor. Add butter; using on/off turns, process until coarse meal forms. Whisk 1 egg and 1 teaspoon cold water in small bowl; add to flour mixture. Using on/off turns, process just until moist clumps form. Transfer to work surface; knead gently until dough comes together, about 4 turns. Form into ball; flatten into disk. Wrap in plastic and chill 1 hour. (*Dough can be made 1 day ahead. Keep chilled.*)

Butter 9½-inch round fluted tart pan with removable bottom. Roll out dough on lightly floured surface to 12-inch round. Transfer dough to pan, pressing onto bottom and up sides of pan; trim any excess dough. Chill 1 hour.

Preheat oven to 400°F. Butter large square of foil and press, butter side down, onto crust. Fill with pie weights or dried beans. Bake 20 minutes. Remove foil and weights. Using fork, pierce bottom of crust all over (about 10 times). Bake until golden, about 10 minutes. Brush with egg white. Cool. (*Can be baked 6 hours ahead. Let stand at room temperature.*)

FOR FILLING: Melt butter in large nonstick skillet over medium heat. Add shallots; sauté until soft, about 2 minutes. Add mushrooms; sprinkle with salt and pepper. Increase heat to high and sauté until liquid is absorbed and mushrooms are tender, about 8 minutes. Sprinkle with 2½ teaspoons thyme and cook 1 minute. Transfer mixture to plate. Cool mushrooms completely.

Preheat oven to 350°F. Place cooled crust in pan on baking sheet. Sprinkle crust with remaining 2½ teaspoons thyme. Drain mushrooms, if needed. Scatter mushrooms over thyme. Whisk cream, eggs, salt, and pepper in medium bowl. Pour egg mixture over mushrooms. Sprinkle with green onions and cheese.

Bake quiche until custard is set, about 25 minutes. Cool 15 minutes. Serve warm or at room temperature.

4 TO 6 SERVINGS

Muenster Cheese Soufflé with Red Bell Pepper and Tomato Salad

1¼ cups whole milk
1½ tablespoons butter
  3 tablespoons all purpose flour
  ¼ teaspoon ground cumin

  Panko (Japanese breadcrumbs)*
  3 large eggs, separated
  1 cup ⅓-inch cubes rindless French Muenster cheese (about 4 ounces)

  Red Bell Pepper and Tomato Salad (see recipe)

Bring milk just to simmer in small saucepan; remove from heat. Melt butter in heavy medium saucepan over medium heat. Whisk in flour; cook roux 2 minutes, whisking constantly (do not brown). Gradually whisk in warm milk. Cook until sauce is smooth and thick enough to drop from whisk in thin ribbon, whisking constantly, about 8 minutes. Remove from heat. Mix in cumin and season generously with salt and pepper; transfer to medium bowl. Cool 10 minutes. (*Soufflé base can be made ahead. Press plastic wrap onto surface. Let stand 2 hours or chill 1 day. Bring to room temperature before using.*)

Preheat oven to 400°F. Butter 4- to 5-cup soufflé dish; coat inside with panko. Whisk egg yolks into soufflé base 1 at a time; stir in cheese cubes. Beat egg whites and pinch of salt in another medium bowl until stiff but not dry. Fold egg whites into soufflé base in 3 additions; transfer to prepared dish.

Bake soufflé until puffed, brown on top, and firm but jiggly to touch, about 28 minutes. Spoon soufflé onto 4 plates. Arrange salad alongside and serve.

Available at some supermarkets and at Asian markets.

2 SERVINGS

Real French Muenster (available at specialty foods stores) will make a big difference in this soufflé. To cube the soft cheese, pare off the rind, then cut cheese into ⅓-inch slices. Freeze slices 15 minutes to firm, then cut into small cubes. Separate cubes on plate and chill. Round out the menu with a dry white wine with plenty of perfume, like Gewürztraminer.

Red Bell Pepper and Tomato Salad

24	grape or cherry tomatoes, halved
½	cup ¼-inch cubes red bell pepper
⅓	cup ¼-inch cubes drained roasted red pepper from jar
3	tablespoons extra-virgin olive oil
½	teaspoon white wine vinegar
	Pinch of ground cumin

Combine all ingredients in medium bowl. Season salad with salt and pepper. (*Can be made 3 hours ahead. Let stand at room temperature, tossing occasionally.*)

2 SERVINGS

Fried Eggs on Toast with Pepper Jack and Avocado

3	tablespoons butter, room temperature, divided
4	large eggs
4	slices hot pepper Monterey Jack cheese
4	½-inch-thick slices country bread, toasted
1	ripe avocado, peeled, pitted, sliced
	Chopped fresh cilantro

Preheat broiler. Melt 1 tablespoon butter in heavy large broilerproof skillet over medium heat. Crack eggs into skillet; sprinkle with salt and pepper. Cook until egg whites are just set on bottom, about 2 minutes. Remove skillet from heat; top each egg with 1 cheese slice. Broil until cheese just melts, about 1 minute.

Spread remaining 2 tablespoons butter on toast; top with eggs, then avocado slices. Sprinkle with cilantro.

4 SERVINGS

Spaghettini with Spicy Escarole and Pecorino Romano

4 tablespoons extra-virgin olive oil, divided
3 anchovy fillets, chopped
¾ teaspoon dried crushed red pepper
2 garlic cloves, minced
1½ pounds escarole (about 1 large head), cut into 1- to 2-inch strips
1 cup water
1 pound spaghettini
Freshly grated Pecorino Romano cheese

PASTA & PIZZA

Heat 2 tablespoons oil in heavy large saucepan over medium heat. Add anchovies and dried crushed red pepper; stir 1 minute. Add garlic; stir 30 seconds. Stir in escarole. Add 1 cup water, cover pan, and reduce heat to low. Cook until escarole is tender, about 5 minutes. Season to taste with salt and pepper.

Meanwhile, cook pasta in large pot of boiling salted water until tender but still firm to bite. Drain pasta, reserving 1 cup cooking liquid. Add pasta to escarole mixture and stir over low heat to combine, adding cooking liquid by tablespoonfuls to moisten if necessary. Stir in 2 tablespoons oil. Divide pasta among shallow bowls, sprinkle with cheese, and serve.

4 TO 6 SERVINGS

The simplicity of this pasta dish lets the slightly nutty and bitter flavor of the escarole shine. To prep the greens, cut the leaves into strips and place them in a large basin of cold water, then dry them in a salad spinner.

Pasta with Eggplant, Basil, and Ricotta Salata

2 medium eggplants (about 1 pound each), cut into ½-inch cubes
2 tablespoons coarse kosher salt plus additional for cooking pasta

5 tablespoons extra-virgin olive oil, divided
1 cup chopped onion
4 garlic cloves, minced
8 (or more) small peperoncini, minced
2 14½-ounce cans diced tomatoes in juice

1 pound spaghetti
1 cup torn fresh basil leaves
1 cup crumbled ricotta salata*

Place eggplant cubes in colander and sprinkle with 2 tablespoons kosher salt. Let eggplant drain 15 minutes. Pat dry, removing excess salt.

Meanwhile, heat 2 tablespoons oil in heavy large skillet over medium heat. Add onion and garlic; sauté until onion is soft, about 5 minutes. Add peperoncini and tomatoes with juice; cook until tomatoes begin to soften, about 15 minutes. Remove tomato sauce from heat.

Heat 1 tablespoon olive oil in another heavy large skillet over high heat. Working in 3 batches and adding 1 tablespoon olive oil for each batch, cook eggplant until browned on all sides, about 8 minutes. Using slotted spoon, transfer eggplant to tomato sauce in skillet.

Meanwhile, cook spaghetti in large pot of boiling salted water until tender but still firm to bite. Drain, reserving 1 cup pasta cooking water. Add cooking water to sauce; bring to boil. Add spaghetti and basil to sauce and toss to coat. Season to taste with salt and pepper. Transfer pasta to bowl; top with ricotta salata and serve.

A salted, dry ricotta cheese; available at some supermarkets, Italian markets, and specialty foods stores.

6 SERVINGS

Pappardelle with Pancetta, Broccoli Rabe, and Pine Nuts

- 4 tablespoons extra-virgin olive oil, divided
- 3 garlic cloves, peeled, flattened
- 1 medium onion, chopped
- 3 ounces thinly sliced pancetta (Italian bacon), chopped
- 1 teaspoon fennel seeds, crushed
- ¾ teaspoon dried crushed red pepper
- 1 large bunch broccoli rabe (also called rapini; generous 1 pound), stems sliced ½ inch thick, tops cut into 2-inch pieces
- 1 cup water
- 1 8.8-ounce package dried pappardelle pasta
- 1 cup freshly grated Pecorino Romano cheese plus additional for serving
- ½ cup pine nuts, toasted

Heat 2 tablespoons oil in heavy large skillet over medium-high heat. Add garlic and cook until golden brown, stirring frequently, about 3 minutes. Discard garlic. Add onion, pancetta, and fennel seeds to skillet; sauté until onion is tender and pancetta begins to brown, about 8 minutes. Add dried crushed red pepper, then broccoli rabe stems and cook 4 minutes to soften slightly, stirring occasionally. Stir in broccoli rabe tops, sprinkle with salt, and add 1 cup water. Cover and cook until stems and tops are tender, about 5 minutes. Season to taste with salt and pepper.

Meanwhile, cook pasta in large pot of boiling salted water until just tender but still firm to bite, stirring occasionally. Drain pasta, reserving 1 cup cooking liquid.

Add pasta to skillet with broccoli rabe and stir over low heat to combine, adding reserved cooking liquid by tablespoonfuls to moisten if necessary. Stir in remaining 2 tablespoons oil and 1 cup cheese. Season to taste with salt and generous amount of pepper. Transfer to large shallow bowl. Sprinkle with pine nuts and serve, passing additional grated cheese separately.

4 SERVINGS

Pasta Party for 8

Antipasto Platter

Breadsticks

Pappardelle with Pancetta, Broccoli Rabe, and Pine Nuts
(double recipe; at left; pictured opposite)

Tricolore Salad

Three-Cheese Garlic Bread
(page 162)

Pinot Grigio

Strawberry Tiramisù
(page 212)

Spaghetti with Asparagus, Shiitake Mushrooms, Lemon, and Chives

12 ounces spaghetti

4 tablespoons butter, divided
2 tablespoons extra-virgin olive oil
½ cup thinly sliced shallots (about 4)
1 pound fresh shiitake mushrooms, stemmed, sliced
6 tablespoons fresh lemon juice
1¾ cups vegetable broth
1 tablespoon grated lemon peel
1 pound asparagus, tough ends trimmed, cut crosswise into thirds
¾ cup chopped fresh chives

4 ounces shaved Asiago cheese*

Cook spaghetti in large pot of boiling salted water until tender but still firm to bite, stirring occasionally. Drain. Transfer pasta to large wide bowl.

Meanwhile, melt 2 tablespoons butter with oil in heavy large skillet over medium heat. Add shallots; sauté 1 minute. Add shiitake mushrooms; sprinkle with salt and pepper. Sauté shiitake mixture until soft, about 6 minutes. Add lemon juice; cook 1 minute. Add

vegetable broth and lemon peel and bring to boil. Reduce heat to medium and simmer until liquid is reduced by half, about 6 minutes. Add asparagus to shiitake mixture; simmer until asparagus turns bright green, about 2 minutes. Add chives and remaining 2 tablespoons butter and stir until butter melts. Season sauce to taste with salt and pepper.

Pour sauce over pasta; toss to coat. Top with shaved Asiago and serve.

*Available at some supermarkets and at Italian markets and specialty foods stores.

4 TO 6 SERVINGS

Pasta with Grilled Vegetables and Feta

1 10½-ounce jar feta cheese cubes in oil with herbs and spices
3 bell peppers (1 yellow, 1 orange, and 1 red), seeded, cut into
   ¾-inch-thick strips
1 large red onion, halved through root end, cut into ¾-inch-thick
   wedges with some root left intact
1 12-ounce package cherry tomatoes
2 tablespoons chopped fresh oregano, divided

1 pound castellane (long oval shells) or penne pasta

Prepare barbecue (medium-high heat). Drain all marinade from feta cheese into large bowl. Add bell pepper strips, onion wedges, and cherry tomatoes to marinade in bowl; sprinkle with salt and pepper and toss to coat. Thread cherry tomatoes on skewers. Grill all vegetables until tender and slightly charred, about 15 minutes for onion wedges, 10 minutes for bell pepper strips, and 5 minutes for cherry tomatoes. Return vegetables to same bowl. Sprinkle with 1½ tablespoons oregano; toss to blend.

Meanwhile, cook pasta in large pot of boiling salted water until tender but still firm to bite, stirring occasionally; drain.

Add pasta and feta cheese to bowl with grilled vegetables; toss to coat. Season to taste with salt and pepper. Sprinkle with remaining ½ tablespoon oregano and serve.

6 SERVINGS

Pasta, cheese, and a few vegetables make a quick and easy main course.

Linguine Avgolemono with Artichoke Hearts and Green Beans

3 large egg yolks
¾ cup fresh lemon juice
½ cup whipping cream

12 ounces frozen artichoke hearts
8 ounces green beans, trimmed, cut on diagonal into 2-inch-long pieces
12 ounces linguine

¾ cup freshly grated Parmesan cheese plus additional for serving
¾ cup chopped fresh Italian parsley

Place egg yolks in medium bowl. Gradually whisk in fresh lemon juice, then whipping cream.

Cook artichoke hearts and green beans in large pot of boiling salted water until crisp-tender, about 5 minutes. Using sieve, transfer vegetables from pot to large skillet. Return water to boil. Add pasta; boil until tender but still firm to bite. Drain pasta, reserving 1½ cups cooking liquid.

Add pasta to skillet with vegetables. Whisk ¾ cup cooking liquid into yolk mixture. Add yolk mixture, ¾ cup cheese, and parsley to skillet. Toss over medium heat just until sauce thickens and coats pasta, about 4 minutes, adding more cooking liquid by tablespoonfuls if dry. Season with salt and pepper. Serve immediately, passing additional cheese alongside.

4 SERVINGS

Farfalle with Sausage, Tomatoes, and Cream

  2 tablespoons olive oil
  1 pound sweet Italian sausages, casings removed
  ½ teaspoon dried crushed red pepper
  1 cup chopped onion
  3 garlic cloves, minced
  1 28-ounce can crushed tomatoes with added puree
  ½ cup whipping cream

  1 pound farfalle (bow-tie pasta)
  ½ cup (packed) chopped fresh basil
     Grated Pecorino Romano cheese

Heat oil in large skillet over medium-high heat. Add sausage and crushed red pepper. Sauté until sausage is no longer pink, breaking into chunks, about 5 minutes. Add onion and garlic; sauté 3 minutes. Add tomatoes and cream. Reduce heat to low; simmer until mixture thickens, about 3 minutes. Season with salt and pepper.

Meanwhile, cook pasta in large pot of boiling salted water until tender but still firm to bite. Drain, reserving 1 cup cooking liquid. Return pasta to same pot. Add sausage mixture to pasta; toss over medium heat, adding reserved cooking liquid by ¼ cupfuls if dry. Transfer pasta to serving dish. Sprinkle with basil. Serve, passing cheese separately.

6 SERVINGS

Mac and Cheese with Chicken and Broccoli

1 pound skinless boneless chicken breasts
Olive oil (for brushing)
2 heads of broccoli, cut into florets (about 5 cups)

2 tablespoons (¼ stick) unsalted butter
2 tablespoons all purpose flour
4 cups whipping cream
1 cup grated Fontina cheese (about 4 ounces)
1 cup grated cheddar cheese (about 4 ounces)
1 pound pasta shells, freshly cooked
½ bunch fresh chives, chopped

Prepare barbecue (medium heat). Sprinkle chicken with salt and pepper. Brush both sides with oil. Grill until cooked through, about 6 minutes per side. Dice chicken and set aside. Cook broccoli in medium pot of boiling salted water until crisp-tender, about 3 minutes.

Melt butter in heavy large saucepan over medium heat. Add flour; stir 2 minutes. Gradually mix in cream. Bring to boil, reduce heat, and simmer 10 minutes, stirring often. Add both cheeses; stir until sauce is smooth. Season with salt and pepper. Add pasta, chicken, and broccoli to sauce; mix well. Garnish with chives.

6 SERVINGS

Fettuccine with Walnuts, Zucchini Ribbons, and Pecorino Romano

2½ pounds small zucchini, untrimmed
1 teaspoon fleur de sel or coarse kosher salt

2 garlic cloves, pressed
2 anchovy fillets, minced (about 1 tablespoon)
½ teaspoon (scant) dried crushed red pepper

1 pound fettuccine
⅓ cup extra-virgin olive oil plus additional for serving
¾ cup walnuts, toasted, coarsely chopped
1 cup freshly grated Pecorino Romano cheese, divided
½ cup (packed) thinly sliced fresh basil
¾ cup (packed) chopped fresh mint
Fresh zucchini flowers, thinly sliced (optional)

Place 1 zucchini on work surface. Using vegetable peeler and firmly holding zucchini by stem end, shave zucchini lengthwise into long ribbons. Discard scraps. Repeat with remaining zucchini. Place ribbons (about 10 cups total) in large colander set over large bowl; sprinkle with 1 teaspoon fleur de sel. Let stand 30 minutes. Rinse zucchini under cold running water; drain well. Spread on 2 large kitchen towels; roll up in towels to absorb excess water. Set aside.

Combine garlic, anchovy fillets, and crushed red pepper in very large serving bowl. Using pestle or wooden spoon, crush mixture until paste forms.

Cook pasta in large pot of boiling salted water until just tender but still firm to bite. Drain, reserving ½ cup cooking liquid. Transfer pasta to bowl with garlic mixture. Add ⅓ cup oil and ¼ cup reserved cooking liquid; toss. Add zucchini, walnuts, ½ cup cheese, basil, and mint; toss. Season with salt and pepper, adding more pasta cooking liquid if mixture is dry. Drizzle with additional oil. Sprinkle with zucchini flowers, if desired. Serve with remaining cheese alongside.

6 SERVINGS

Grilled Chorizo, Goat Cheese, and Watercress Pita Pizzas

14 ounces fresh pork or beef chorizo sausages, plastic casings removed
4 cups (packed) watercress tops, divided
8 ounces soft fresh goat cheese, crumbled

8 5- to 6-inch-diameter pita breads
Olive oil
3 mini sweet peppers (1 yellow, 1 orange, and 1 red), cut into thin rings

Prepare barbecue (medium heat). Sauté chorizo in large skillet over medium-high heat until cooked through, breaking up with spoon, about 8 minutes. Transfer chorizo to sieve set over bowl and drain. Mix 2½ cups watercress and goat cheese in medium bowl.

Lightly brush 1 side of each pita bread with oil. Grill, oiled side down, until bottom is just crisp, about 2 minutes. Transfer to work surface, grilled side up. Cover each pita bread with cheese mixture, chorizo, and several sweet pepper rings, dividing equally.

Return pita pizzas to barbecue. Grill, covered, until goat cheese softens, about 2 minutes. Transfer pita pizzas to serving platter. Top each with more watercress and serve.

MAKES 8

Double-Cheese and Prosciutto Calzone

> 2 cups grated mozzarella cheese (about 8 ounces)
> 3½ ounces soft fresh goat cheese, crumbled
> 2 ounces prosciutto slices, chopped
> 2½ teaspoons chopped fresh thyme
> 1 garlic clove, pressed
> 1 13.8-ounce tube refrigerated pizza dough
> Extra-virgin olive oil

Position rack in middle of oven; preheat to 425°F. Toss first 5 ingredients in medium bowl. Season with pepper. Unroll dough into rectangle on rimmed baking sheet. Mound filling crosswise on lower half of dough, leaving 1-inch border on sides. Fold upper half of dough over. Crimp edges to seal; fold corners under to form half-circle. Bake until puffed and brown, about 18 minutes. Brush with oil. Transfer to platter and cut into 4 pieces.

4 SERVINGS

Using purchased pizza dough to make one large calzone saves lots of time. For a lower-calorie, lower-fat calzone, use part-skim mozzarella.

Iceberg Wedge with Warm Bacon and
Blue Cheese Dressing (page 142)

On the Side

Side Dishes

Salads

Breads

Red Beans and Rice

3 bacon slices, chopped
1 cup chopped onion
¾ cup chopped red bell pepper
4 garlic cloves, minced
3 cups long-grain white rice
3 bay leaves
2 tablespoons tomato paste
1 tablespoon ground cumin
1 tablespoon hot Spanish smoked paprika (Pimentón de la Vera)
2 teaspoons salt
4 cups water
1 15- to 15½-ounce can kidney beans, rinsed, drained

Sauté chopped bacon in heavy 4-quart saucepan over medium-high heat until bacon is brown and fat is rendered, about 5 minutes. Add onion, red bell pepper, and garlic; sauté until onion is golden, about 5 minutes. Add rice and stir until coated, about 1 minute. Stir in bay leaves, tomato paste, cumin, paprika, and salt. Add 4 cups water and beans and bring to boil. Reduce heat to medium-low; cover and cook until rice is tender and liquid is absorbed, about 18 minutes. Remove from heat; let stand covered 10 minutes. Fluff rice with fork. Remove bay leaves. Transfer rice to bowl and serve.

8 SERVINGS

Thyme-Roasted Carrots

2 pounds medium carrots, peeled, cut on deep diagonal into ½-inch-thick slices
1½ tablespoons olive oil
1½ teaspoons fresh thyme leaves
1½ tablespoons butter

Preheat oven to 400°F. Toss carrots, oil, and thyme in large bowl. Sprinkle generously with salt and pepper. Spread carrots in single layer on large rimmed baking sheet; dot with butter. Roast until carrots are tender and brown, stirring occasionally, about 40 minutes.

6 SERVINGS

SIDE DISHES

Mozzarella-Stuffed Grilled Portobellos with Balsamic Marinade

¼ cup extra-virgin olive oil

2 tablespoons plus 1 teaspoon balsamic vinegar

3 garlic cloves, minced, divided

6 large portobello mushrooms, stemmed

1½ cups panko (Japanese breadcrumbs)*

1 cup shredded mozzarella cheese (about 5 ounces)

½ cup grated Parmesan cheese (about 2 ounces)

¼ cup chopped green onions

1½ teaspoons chopped fresh oregano

1½ teaspoons chopped fresh thyme

¼ cup (½ stick) butter, melted

Whisk oil, 2 tablespoons vinegar, and 1 garlic clove in small bowl for marinade. Using spoon, scrape out gills from mushrooms and place mushrooms on rimmed baking sheet. Brush marinade over both sides of mushrooms, arrange hollow side up, and let stand at room temperature 30 minutes.

Prepare barbecue (medium heat). Mix panko, next 5 ingredients, and remaining 2 garlic cloves in medium bowl. Drizzle butter and remaining teaspoon vinegar over panko mixture and toss. Divide panko mixture among mushrooms, leaving ½-inch border around edges and packing down slightly. Place mushrooms on grill, stuffing side up; cover grill and cook until cheese melts and juices bubble at edges of mushrooms, rearranging mushrooms occasionally for even cooking (do not turn over), about 6 minutes.

Sold in the Asian foods section of some supermarkets and at Asian markets.

MAKES 6

Orzo with Tomatoes, Feta, and Green Onions

¼ cup red wine vinegar
2 tablespoons fresh lemon juice
1 teaspoon honey
½ cup olive oil

6 cups chicken broth
1 pound orzo

2 cups red and yellow teardrop or grape tomatoes, halved
1 7-ounce package feta cheese, cut into ½-inch cubes (about 1½ cups)
1 cup chopped fresh basil
1 cup chopped green onions
½ cup pine nuts, toasted

Whisk vinegar, lemon juice, and honey in small bowl. Gradually whisk in oil. Season vinaigrette with salt and pepper. *(Can be made 2 days ahead. Cover and chill.)*

Bring broth to boil in heavy large saucepan. Stir in orzo, reduce heat to medium, and cover partially; boil until tender but still firm to bite, stirring occasionally. Drain. Transfer to large wide bowl, tossing frequently until cool.

Mix tomatoes, feta, basil, and green onions into orzo. Add vinaigrette; toss to coat. Season with salt and pepper. *(Can be made 2 hours ahead. Let stand at room temperature.)* Add pine nuts and toss to combine. Serve at room temperature.

8 SERVINGS

Spring Dinner for 8

Stuffed Artichokes

Roast Leg of Lamb with
Salsa Verde
(page 56)

Orzo with Tomatoes, Feta, and
Green Onions
(at left)

Spring Greens with
Orange-Fennel Vinaigrette
(page 153)

Zinfandel

Lemon Cloud Tart with
Rhubarb Compote
(page 172)

Pan-Fried Jerusalem Artichokes in Sage Butter

- 3 tablespoons butter, divided
- 2 tablespoons olive oil
- 1 pound Jerusalem artichokes,* scrubbed, cut crosswise into ¼-inch-thick rounds
- 3 tablespoons coarsely torn fresh sage leaves, divided
- 2 teaspoons fresh lemon juice
- 2 tablespoons chopped fresh Italian parsley

Melt 1 tablespoon butter with olive oil in large nonstick skillet over medium-high heat. Add Jerusalem artichokes and half of sage. Sprinkle with salt and pepper. Sauté until brown and just beginning to soften, turning frequently, about 10 minutes. Using slotted spoon, transfer Jerusalem artichokes to shallow serving bowl. Add remaining 2 tablespoons butter and sage to skillet; fry until sage darkens and begins to crisp, about 30 seconds. Add lemon juice; simmer 1 minute. Pour lemon-sage butter over Jerusalem artichokes in bowl, tossing to coat. Season with salt and pepper. Sprinkle with parsley and serve.

The tubers of a North American sunflower, Jerusalem artichokes (also labeled "sunchokes") are available in the produce section of many supermarkets.

4 TO 6 SERVINGS

Jerusalem artichokes are a nutty-earthy root vegetable and they taste great when they're pan-fried in sage butter. But to be picky, they're tubers, not artichokes, and they come from North America, not the Middle East.

Fresh Corn Sauté with Tomatoes, Squash, and Fried Okra

½ cup yellow cornmeal
¼ teaspoon (or more) cayenne pepper
12 okra pods, cut crosswise into ½-inch pieces

6 tablespoons olive oil, divided
2 cups fresh corn kernels (cut from about 3 ears of corn)
6 baby green pattypan squash, each cut into 6 pieces
2 garlic cloves, chopped
1 12-ounce bag cherry tomatoes, halved (2 cups)
2 tablespoons chopped fresh cilantro
2 green onions, chopped

Tossing the okra in cornmeal before frying creates a crisp coating, adding texture to this colorful dish.

Mix cornmeal and ¼ teaspoon cayenne in small bowl. Add okra and toss lightly to coat. Pour okra into sieve; shake off excess cornmeal.

Heat 4 tablespoons oil in heavy large skillet over medium heat. Add okra and sauté until coating is golden brown, stirring occasionally, about 6 minutes. Using slotted spoon, transfer okra to paper towels to drain; sprinkle with salt and pepper. Wipe out skillet. Heat remaining 2 tablespoons oil in same skillet over medium heat. Add corn, squash, and garlic; sauté 2 minutes. Add tomatoes; cover and cook until squash is crisp-tender, about 5 minutes. Mix in okra, cilantro, and green onions. Remove from heat. Season to taste with salt, pepper, and more cayenne, if desired.

4 TO 6 SERVINGS

"Soda Jerk" Beans

2 cups ½-inch cubes cooked ham
1 15-ounce can diced tomatoes in juice, drained
1 15-ounce can pork and beans, rinsed, drained
1 15-ounce can black beans, rinsed, drained
1 15-ounce can butter beans, rinsed, drained
1 15-ounce can pinto beans, rinsed, drained
1 large onion, chopped
1 large red bell pepper, chopped
1 large green bell pepper, chopped
½ cup (packed) dark brown sugar
½ cup cola-flavored soda
½ cup lemon-lime soda
2 teaspoons curry powder
½ teaspoon dried savory
½ teaspoon garlic powder
¼ teaspoon cayenne pepper

Place all ingredients in heavy large pot. Bring to boil over medium-high heat, stirring until sugar dissolves. Reduce heat to medium and simmer uncovered until juices are thick, stirring gently and frequently to prevent burning, about 20 minutes. Season with salt and pepper.

MAKES ABOUT 10 CUPS

Spring Vegetable Fricassee with Saffron Cream

2 cups baby carrots (about 3 bunches), tops removed, scrubbed
1 cup shelled fresh peas or frozen peas, thawed

1 tablespoon olive oil
1 small onion, thinly sliced
2 shallots, thinly sliced
1 leek (white part only), halved, thinly sliced
½ teaspoon (scant) saffron threads
¾ cup fresh morel mushrooms
1 teaspoon chopped fresh thyme
½ cup dry white wine
⅔ cup vegetable broth
1⅓ cups whipping cream
½ pound asparagus, tough ends trimmed, cut crosswise into thirds
4 cups baby spinach leaves (about 3 ounces)

Preheat oven to 350°F. Lightly butter 1-quart baking dish. Cook carrots in large pot of boiling salted water 2 minutes. Using slotted spoon, transfer carrots to bowl of ice water to cool. Using slotted spoon, transfer carrots to medium bowl. (If using fresh peas, cook in same pot of boiling water 2 minutes; drain and transfer to bowl of ice water to cool. Using slotted spoon, transfer peas to small bowl. If using frozen peas, add later, according to recipe.)

Heat oil in medium saucepan over medium heat. Add onion; sauté 1 minute. Add shallots; sauté 1 minute. Add leek and sauté until vegetables are soft, about 4 minutes longer (do not brown). Stir in saffron. Add carrots, mushrooms, and thyme. Season with salt and pepper. Add wine and simmer until almost dry, about 3 minutes. Add broth and simmer 4 minutes. Add cream and bring to simmer. Stir in peas, asparagus, and spinach. Transfer to prepared baking dish and bake until edges are bubbling and top begins to brown, about 30 minutes.

4 SERVINGS

Morel mushrooms lend an earthy note to this beautiful side dish. Sponge-like, they can trap grit, so wash them in a bowl of cool water, scoop them out carefully, and pat dry. Or you can use dried morels. Start with ½ ounce of dried morels; cover with ½ cup boiling water. Let soak until soft, about 20 minutes. Using a slotted spoon, transfer mushrooms to small bowl. Add soaking liquid to carrot-saffron mixture (leaving sediment behind) after evaporating wine. Boil until almost dry, about 5 minutes before adding broth.

Grilled Zucchini with Garlic and Lemon Butter Baste

- 8 medium zucchini (about 2½ pounds), trimmed, halved lengthwise
- ½ cup (1 stick) butter
- 1 tablespoon frozen unsweetened lemon juice concentrate or 2 tablespoons fresh lemon juice
- 1 teaspoon lemon-pepper seasoning
- 1 teaspoon garlic powder
- 1 teaspoon dried oregano
- ¼ teaspoon curry powder
- ¼ cup grated Parmesan cheese (optional)

Preheat barbecue (medium heat). Score cut side of zucchini halves diagonally about ¼ inch deep at 1-inch intervals. Melt butter with lemon juice concentrate, lemon-pepper seasoning, garlic powder, oregano, and curry powder in heavy small saucepan. Season with salt and pepper. Brush seasoned butter on cut side of zucchini. Place zucchini on grill and cook until charred on all sides and just beginning to soften, about 12 minutes. If desired, arrange zucchini on grill, cut side up, and sprinkle with cheese; close lid of barbecue and cook until cheese just softens, about 1 minute. Transfer zucchini to platter.

8 SERVINGS

Fennel Mashed Potatoes

- 2 tablespoons (¼ stick) butter
- 1 fennel bulb, trimmed, quartered, cored, thinly sliced crosswise
- ½ teaspoon fennel seeds, crushed
- 2½ pounds russet potatoes or Yukon Gold potatoes, peeled, cut into 2-inch pieces
- 1 cup (or more) half and half

Melt butter in heavy large skillet over medium heat. Add sliced fennel bulb and crushed fennel seeds and stir to coat. Sprinkle with salt and pepper. Reduce heat to low, cover, and cook until fennel is tender but not brown, stirring often, about 20 minutes. (*Can be made 2 hours ahead. Let stand at room temperature.*)

Place potatoes in large saucepan. Cover with cold water and bring to boil. Reduce heat to medium and boil until potatoes are tender, about 15 minutes. Drain. Return potatoes to pan; cook over medium heat until no liquid remains. Mash potatoes.

Add 1 cup half and half to fennel mixture and bring to simmer. Working in 2 batches, add fennel mixture to potatoes; stir to combine. Season with salt and pepper. *(Can be made 2 hours ahead. Let stand at room temperature. Rewarm over medium heat, adding more half and half as needed if dry.)*

6 SERVINGS

Baked Garden Tomatoes with Cheese

      2   tablespoons extra-virgin olive oil
      3   garlic cloves, chopped
      1   medium onion, chopped
    1¾   pounds fresh vine-ripened or heirloom tomatoes, cut into ½-inch
           pieces
      3   tablespoons chopped fresh chives
      1   cup (packed) freshly grated Parmesan cheese
      1   cup (packed) freshly grated Romano cheese

Preheat oven to 350°F. Oil 11x7-inch baking dish. Heat 2 tablespoons oil in heavy large skillet over medium heat. Add garlic and sauté until fragrant, about 30 seconds. Add onion and sauté until soft, about 6 minutes. Add tomatoes, reduce heat to medium-low, and cook until beginning to soften, about 5 minutes. Mix in chives; season with salt and pepper. Transfer tomato mixture to prepared baking dish; sprinkle grated cheeses over. Bake until cheese melts and begins to turn golden brown, about 20 minutes.

6 SERVINGS

Farmers' Market Dinner for 8

Gazpacho

Grilled Steak with Fresh Garden Herbs
(double recipe; page 40)

Grilled Zucchini with Garlic and Lemon Butter Baste
(opposite; pictured opposite)

Roasted New Potatoes

Cabernet Sauvignon

Peach and Mascarpone Cheesecake with Balsamic Syrup
(page 198)

Grilled Japanese Eggplant with Feta and Sun-Dried Tomatoes

    12 Japanese eggplants, stemmed, halved lengthwise
     1 tablespoon salt

    ⅓   cup chopped drained oil-packed sun-dried tomatoes
    ¼   cup fresh lemon juice
     2 tablespoons olive oil plus more for grilling
     2 garlic cloves, minced
     1 tablespoon chopped fresh Italian parsley plus whole sprigs for garnish
     1 tablespoon chopped fresh mint plus whole sprigs for garnish
     1 cup (packed) crumbled feta cheese

Place eggplant halves in large colander. Toss with salt. Let stand 30 minutes. Transfer to paper towels; pat dry.

Meanwhile, stir tomatoes, lemon juice, 2 tablespoons oil, garlic, chopped parsley, and chopped mint in medium bowl. Mix in cheese. Season topping with salt and pepper. (*Can be made 3 hours ahead. Cover and chill.*)

Prepare barbecue (medium-high heat). Brush eggplant with oil. Grill until tender, about 3 minutes per side. Place on platter, cut side up. Spoon on feta topping. Garnish with parsley and mint sprigs and serve.

12 SERVINGS

Broccoli Pancotto

     3 cups 1-inch cubes crustless country-style bread

    ¼   cup extra-virgin olive oil
     3 small dried chiles de árbol*
     2 large garlic cloves, peeled, flattened
     1 pound broccoli crowns, cut into florets (about 7 cups)
    ½   cup water

Preheat oven to 375°F. Arrange bread on baking sheet. Bake until beginning to brown, about 12 minutes. Cool on sheet.

Heat oil in large skillet over medium heat. Add chiles and garlic; sauté until fragrant, about 2 minutes. Add broccoli florets, ½ cup water, and bread. Cook uncovered until bread absorbs water and broccoli is crisp-tender, stirring often, about 15 minutes. Season to taste with salt and pepper.

*Bright red chiles that are sold at some supermarkets, specialty foods stores, and Latin markets.

6 SERVINGS

Sweet-Hot BBQ Tater Fries

2 pounds sweet potatoes or yams, peeled, cut lengthwise into ½-inch-thick slices, each slice cut lengthwise into ½-inch-wide strips
¼ cup extra-virgin olive oil
1 tablespoon chopped fresh rosemary
1 tablespoon (packed) golden brown sugar
1 teaspoon garlic powder
¼ teaspoon cayenne pepper
Additional olive oil

Prepare barbecue (medium heat). Place potatoes in 13x9x2-inch baking dish. Add ¼ cup oil, chopped fresh rosemary, brown sugar, garlic powder, and cayenne pepper to potatoes. Sprinkle potatoes with salt and pepper; toss to coat. Brush grill lightly with oil. Place potatoes on grill, spacing about 1 inch apart. Grill until potatoes are tender and slightly charred, turning occasionally, about 10 minutes total. Transfer potatoes to bowl, season to taste with salt and pepper, and serve.

4 TO 6 SERVINGS

Backyard Barbecue for 6

Ranch Dip with Crudités

Bourbon-Glazed Baby Back Ribs
(page 64)

Sweet-Hot BBQ Tater Fries
(at left; pictured at left)

Iceberg Wedge with Warm Bacon and Blue Cheese Dressing
(page 142)

Zinfandel and ***Beer***

Peach and Blackberry Shortcakes with Blackberry Cream
(page 180)

Parsnip and Hazelnut Gratin with Sage

4 ounces bacon slices, chopped
2 pounds parsnips (about 11 medium), peeled, trimmed, thinly sliced lengthwise
½ cup hazelnuts, chopped, toasted, divided
2 cups whipping cream
1 cup low-salt chicken broth
1½ teaspoons kosher salt
1 teaspoon ground black pepper

2 tablespoons minced fresh sage

Preheat oven to 400°F. Sauté bacon in heavy medium skillet over medium-high heat until golden brown, about 6 minutes. Using slotted spoon, transfer bacon to large bowl. Stir in parsnips and ¼ cup hazelnuts. Arrange mixture in even layer in 2-quart baking dish. Combine cream, broth, salt, and pepper in medium bowl. Pour over parsnip mixture.

Bake gratin 30 minutes. Press down on parsnips with spatula to moisten evenly. Continue baking until parsnips are tender and liquid bubbles thickly, about 35 minutes longer. Let stand 10 minutes. Sprinkle with remaining hazelnuts and sage.

8 TO 10 SERVINGS

Green-Onion Risotto

- 4 cups (or more) low-salt chicken broth
- 2 tablespoons (¼ stick) butter
- 1 bunch green onions, white parts finely chopped, green parts thinly sliced
- 1 cup arborio or medium-grain rice
- ½ cup dry white wine
- ¼ cup freshly grated Parmesan cheese
- 2 tablespoons mascarpone cheese or whipping cream
- 1 teaspoon finely grated orange peel

Bring chicken broth to simmer in medium saucepan over medium heat. Reduce heat to low and keep both warm.

Melt butter in large saucepan over medium heat. Add chopped green onions and cook until soft, stirring often, about 6 minutes. Stir in rice. Add wine; cook until almost all liquid is absorbed, stirring frequently, about 2 minutes. Add 4 cups broth, 1 cup at a time, cooking until almost all broth is absorbed before adding more, stirring frequently, until rice is tender but still firm, about 20 minutes. Stir in sliced green onions, Parmesan, mascarpone, and orange peel. Add more broth by ¼ cupfuls as needed if dry. Season with salt and pepper.

4 SERVINGS

Asparagus with Bacon and Onion

- 3 slices bacon, cut into ¼-inch pieces
- ½ small onion, cut into ¼-inch cubes
- 2 teaspoons hazelnut oil or walnut oil
- 1 teaspoon fresh lemon juice
- 24 stalks of asparagus, trimmed

Cook bacon in large skillet until crisp; transfer to paper towels. Pour off all but 1 teaspoon drippings from skillet. Return bacon to skillet; mix in onion. Remove from heat. Whisk oil and lemon juice in small bowl; season with salt and pepper.

Cook asparagus in pot of boiling salted water until crisp-tender, about 3 minutes. Transfer to paper towels to drain, then place in large bowl. Add dressing; toss. Arrange on platter. Stir bacon mixture over medium-low heat about 3 minutes; spoon atop asparagus.

4 SERVINGS

Saturday Night Dinner Party for 10

Cauliflower Soup with Seared Scallops, Lemon Oil, and Caviar
(double recipe; page 28)

Pinot Gris

Prime Rib

Parsnip and Hazelnut Gratin with Sage
(opposite; pictured opposite)

Brussels Sprouts with Lemon

Cabernet Sauvignon

Deep Dark Chocolate Cheesecake
(page 188)

Radicchio and Haricot Vert Salad with Candied Walnuts

¾ cup walnut halves

¼ cup (packed) dark brown sugar

2 teaspoons plus ¼ cup walnut oil

3½ tablespoons seasoned rice vinegar, divided

1 garlic clove, pressed

1 head of Bibb lettuce, coarsely torn

½ large head of radicchio, thickly sliced

2 cups frozen haricots verts or small slender green beans, thawed

Combine walnuts, sugar, 2 teaspoons oil, and 1 tablespoon vinegar in medium nonstick skillet. Stir over medium heat until syrup coats nuts thickly, about 2 minutes. Season with salt and pepper. Transfer nuts to piece of foil. Separate nuts; freeze on foil 5 minutes or cool completely at room temperature.

Whisk remaining ¼ cup oil, remaining 2½ tablespoons vinegar, and garlic in large bowl. Season dressing with salt and pepper. Add Bibb lettuce, radicchio, haricots verts, and nuts; toss to coat.

6 TO 8 SERVINGS

Roasted Baby Beets and Arugula Salad with Lemon-Gorgonzola Vinaigrette

¼ cup fresh lemon juice

1 tablespoon red wine vinegar

½ cup plus ⅓ cup extra-virgin olive oil

½ cup crumbled Gorgonzola cheese (about 4 ounces)

2 cups roughly torn bite-size pieces French bread

¼ cup assorted chopped fresh herbs (such as parsley, basil, and rosemary)

1 garlic clove, minced

24 baby beets, trimmed, scrubbed

8 ounces baby arugula (about 12 cups)

Use a milder domestic Gorgonzola, rather than the equally delicious but more pungent Italian version, which would overpower the salad. Select an assortment of different-colored beets to make the salad more vibrant.

Place lemon juice and vinegar in small bowl. Gradually whisk in ½ cup olive oil. Stir in cheese. Season with salt and pepper. (*Dressing can be made 1 day ahead. Cover and refrigerate.*)

Preheat oven to 375°F. Heat remaining ⅓ cup olive oil in medium ovenproof skillet over medium heat. Add bread pieces; toss to coat. Add herbs and garlic; toss to coat. Sauté until bread is crisp, about 4 minutes. Using slotted spoon, transfer croutons to plate in single layer. Cool.

Add beets to same skillet, tossing to coat with any remaining herbs and oil. Cover skillet with foil and transfer to oven. Roast until beets are tender, about 45 minutes. Cool beets. Peel, if desired; cut in half.

Toss arugula with dressing to taste in large wide bowl. Season with salt and pepper. Top with roasted beets and croutons and serve.

6 SERVINGS

Iceberg Wedge with Warm Bacon and Blue Cheese Dressing

1½ cups mayonnaise
2 tablespoons fresh lemon juice
1 tablespoon coarsely ground black pepper
1 teaspoon hot pepper sauce
1 cup coarsely crumbled blue cheese
Buttermilk (optional)

½ pound thick-cut bacon, cut crosswise into 1-inch pieces
1 large head of iceberg lettuce, cut into 6 wedges, each with some core attached
½ red onion, very thinly sliced

Mix first 4 ingredients in medium bowl. Add blue cheese and stir until well blended. If too thick, thin with buttermilk by tablespoonfuls to desired consistency. *(Can be made 1 day ahead. Cover and chill.)*

Cook bacon in large skillet over medium heat until golden brown and beginning to crisp. Arrange lettuce on plates. Spoon dressing over. Using slotted spoon, transfer warm bacon from skillet onto salads, dividing equally. Garnish with red onion.

6 SERVINGS

Heirloom Tomato and Burrata Cheese Salad

4 large heirloom tomatoes (about 2½ pounds) or 4 to 5 large plum tomatoes
Fleur de sel or coarse kosher salt
Freshly ground black pepper
1 teaspoon dried oregano
¼ cup torn fresh basil leaves plus additional whole leaves for garnish
¼ cup extra-virgin olive oil

4 2.5-ounce rounds burrata cheese

Cut tomatoes into wedges and place in large bowl. Sprinkle with fleur de sel and pepper. Crush oregano between palms to release flavor; add to tomatoes. Add ¼ cup basil and oil and mix well. Let stand at room temperature at least 30 minutes and up to 1 hour, stirring occasionally.

Place 1 burrata cheese round in center of each plate. Fan tomatoes around cheese, dividing equally. Drizzle with dressing from bowl. Garnish with additional basil leaves and serve.

4 SERVINGS

Israeli Couscous, Asparagus, Cucumber, and Olive Salad

- 1 garlic clove
- 3 tablespoons fresh lemon juice
- 1 teaspoon Dijon mustard
- ½ cup extra-virgin olive oil

- 2½ cups low-salt chicken broth
- 2 cups toasted Israeli couscous* (about 6 ounces)

- 2 cups ½-inch pieces thin asparagus spears, blanched 2 minutes
- 2 cups ½-inch cubes seeded English hothouse cucumber
- ½ cup pitted Kalamata olives, halved
- 2 large green onions, chopped
- ¼ cup fresh mint leaves plus sprigs for garnish
- 1½ cups coarsely crumbled feta cheese (about 7 ounces)

Press garlic clove into small bowl. Add lemon juice and mustard; whisk in oil. Season dressing with salt and pepper.

Bring broth to boil in heavy medium saucepan. Mix in couscous. Cover, reduce heat to medium-low, and simmer until couscous is tender and broth is absorbed, about 10 minutes. Transfer to large bowl; sprinkle with salt and pepper. Cool to room temperature, tossing occasionally, about 45 minutes.

Mix asparagus, cucumber, olives, green onions, and ¼ cup mint leaves into couscous. Add dressing; toss. Gently mix in cheese. (*Can be made 2 hours ahead. Let stand at room temperature.*) Garnish with mint sprigs.

Israeli couscous is a small, round, toasted pasta. Look for it in the pasta and grains section of the supermarket or at Middle Eastern markets.

8 SERVINGS

Spinach and Celery Salad with Lemon Vinaigrette

    4   large celery stalks, very thinly sliced on diagonal
    6   ounces baby spinach leaves (about 10 cups loosely packed)
  ¼   cup extra-virgin olive oil
    3   tablespoons fresh Meyer lemon juice or regular lemon juice

Combine celery and spinach in large bowl. Drizzle olive oil and lemon juice over; sprinkle generously with salt and pepper and toss to coat.

6 SERVINGS

Green Bean and Radish Salad

    1   pound green beans, trimmed
  15   large red radishes, trimmed, cut into ¼-inch-thick slices
    6   tablespoons olive oil
    2   shallots, chopped
    2   tablespoons red wine vinegar
    2   tablespoons fresh lemon juice

Cook green beans in large pot of boiling salted water until crisp-tender, about 3 minutes. Add radishes and cook 30 seconds longer. Drain beans and radishes. Rinse with cold water; drain well. Combine all ingredients in large bowl and toss to coat. Let marinate 1 hour at room temperature, tossing occasionally. Season to taste with salt and pepper and serve.

4 TO 6 SERVINGS

Tangy Avocado-Orange Salad

    2   oranges
  ½   small head of red leaf lettuce, coarsely torn
    1   small avocado, halved, pitted, peeled, diced
    2   tablespoons white balsamic vinegar

Using small sharp knife, cut off peel and white pith from oranges. Working over large bowl, cut between membranes to release orange segments. Add lettuce, avocado, and vinegar to bowl; toss gently. Season with salt and pepper; divide among 4 plates.

4 SERVINGS

Picnic in the Park for 8

Celery and Carrot Sticks

Lavender Iced Tea
(*page 33*)

Turkey Sandwiches

Israeli Couscous, Asparagus, Cucumber, and Olive Salad
(*opposite; pictured opposite*)

Spiced Coconut Loaf Cake
(*page 193*)

Strawberries

Black-Eyed Pea and Pumpkin Salad

PEAS

1 cup dried black-eyed peas

4 cups water

½ medium onion

1 bay leaf

½ teaspoon salt

PUMPKIN

1½ cups ½-inch cubes seeded peeled sugar pumpkin or butternut squash (about 6 ounces)

3 tablespoons water

1 tablespoon olive oil

1 small garlic clove, minced

SALAD

3 tablespoons extra-virgin olive oil

1½ tablespoons fresh lime juice

1 cup thinly sliced red onion

¼ cup chopped green bell pepper

¼ cup chopped seeded peeled cucumber

1 plum tomato, seeded, chopped

2 tablespoons chopped fresh basil

FOR PEAS: Place peas in large saucepan. Add enough water to cover by 3 inches. Let peas soak 2 hours. Drain peas; return to same pan. Add 4 cups water, onion, bay leaf, and salt. Bring to boil; reduce heat to medium, cover partially, and simmer until peas are tender, about 30 minutes. Discard onion and bay leaf. Drain. Transfer peas to rimmed baking sheet to cool. *(Can be prepared 1 day ahead. Cover and refrigerate.)*

FOR PUMPKIN: Preheat oven to 400°F. Arrange pumpkin in single layer in 8x8x2-inch glass baking dish. Drizzle with 3 tablespoons water and oil. Sprinkle with salt and pepper. Bake until tender when pierced, turning occasionally, about 15 minutes. Add garlic; stir to coat. Cool.

FOR SALAD: Whisk oil and lime juice in bowl. Season dressing with salt and pepper. Combine all remaining ingredients and peas in large bowl. Add dressing; toss. Season with salt and pepper. Add pumpkin and toss to combine. *(Can be made 2 hours ahead. Let stand at room temperature.)*

Red, White, and Blue Potato Salad

   1 cup chopped green onions, divided
   1 cup sour cream
  ½ cup mayonnaise
  ¼ cup white wine vinegar
   4 teaspoons Dijon mustard
   2 teaspoons sugar
   2 teaspoons salt
   1 teaspoon ground black pepper

   1 pound unpeeled small or baby red-skinned potatoes
   1 pound small purple or blue potatoes, peeled
   1 pound unpeeled small white creamer or White Rose potatoes

   2 cups cooked fresh peas, or one 10-ounce package frozen, thawed
1½ cups crumbled blue cheese (about 6 ounces)

   Paprika

Whisk ½ cup green onions and next 7 ingredients in medium bowl. Cover and chill dressing. *(Can be made 1 day ahead. Keep chilled.)*

Place all potatoes in large saucepan. Add enough water to cover by 1 inch. Sprinkle with salt. Bring to boil, reduce heat to medium, and boil until tender, 10 to 15 minutes (time will vary depending on size and variety of potatoes). Drain and cool to room temperature.

Cut potatoes into ½-inch-thick slices and place in large bowl. Add dressing, peas, and blue cheese; toss gently. Cover and refrigerate at least 2 hours and up to 1 day.

Sprinkle potato salad with paprika and ½ cup green onions.

MAKES ABOUT 8 CUPS

Arugula Salad with Dates and Marcona Almonds

Mediterranean Dinner for 10

Phyllo-Cheese Triangles

Grilled Swordfish

Grilled Japanese Eggplant with
Feta and Sun-Dried Tomatoes
(page 136)

Arugula Salad with
Dates and Marcona Almonds
(at left; pictured at left)

Vernaccia

Sticky Date and Almond
Bread Pudding with
Amaretto Zabaglione
(page 206)

10	cups baby arugula (about 5 ounces)
3	tablespoons almond oil or olive oil, divided
1	teaspoon fresh lemon juice
4	large oranges, peeled, cut crosswise into ⅓-inch-thick rounds
15	Medjool dates, halved, pitted
1	small wedge Parmesan cheese, shaved into strips with vegetable peeler
½	cup Marcona almonds,* coarsely chopped

Toss arugula, 1 tablespoon oil, and lemon juice in large bowl until coated; sprinkle with salt and pepper. Mound arugula on platter or in large shallow dish. Top arugula with orange rounds, dates, and cheese strips. Drizzle remaining 2 tablespoons oil over. Sprinkle salad with almonds and serve.

Salted almonds from Spain; sold at natural foods stores and specialty stores.

10 SERVINGS

Rainbow Slaw

1½ cups mayonnaise
2 tablespoons apple cider vinegar
1 tablespoon sugar
1 tablespoon pure maple syrup
1 small green cabbage, thinly sliced (about 8 cups)
1 small red cabbage, thinly sliced (about 8 cups)
2 medium carrots, peeled, grated
1 small yam (red-skinned sweet potato), peeled, grated
1 large unpeeled Fuji apple, cored, grated
1 large unpeeled Golden Delicious apple, cored, grated
1 medium-size green pepper, cored, seeded, thinly sliced
3 green onions, finely chopped
Paprika

Whisk mayonnaise, apple cider vinegar, sugar, and maple syrup in small bowl. Place green cabbage and next 7 ingredients in very large bowl. Pour dressing over; toss. Season to taste with salt and pepper. Cover and chill 1 hour. (*Can be made 8 hours ahead. Chill.*) Sprinkle with paprika and serve.

MAKES ABOUT 8 CUPS

Cantaloupe Salad with Lime, Mint, and Ginger

1 cantaloupe, halved, seeded, peeled
3 tablespoons fresh lime juice
3 tablespoons chopped fresh mint
2 teaspoons grated lime peel
2 tablespoons sugar
2½ teaspoons grated peeled fresh ginger
2 teaspoons honey

Cut cantaloupe into ¾- to 1-inch cubes (about 5 cups) and place in large bowl. Add lime juice, mint, and lime peel; toss to blend. Mix in sugar, ginger, and honey. Refrigerate salad until ready to serve, stirring occasionally, up to 3 hours.

4 TO 6 SERVINGS

Pool Party for 8

Seven-Layer Dip and Chips

Cheeseburgers

"Soda Jerk" Beans
(*page 132*)

Rainbow Slaw
(*at left; pictured opposite*)

Beer and *Limeade*

Jamaican Coffee Brownies
with Pecans
(*page 230*)

Tomato-Watermelon Salad with
Feta and Toasted Almonds

- 8 cups 1¼-inch chunks seedless watermelon (about 6 pounds)
- 3 pounds ripe tomatoes (preferably heirloom) in assorted colors, cored, cut into 1¼-inch chunks (about 6 cups)
- 1 teaspoon (or more) fleur de sel or coarse kosher salt
- 5 tablespoons extra-virgin olive oil, divided
- 1½ tablespoons red wine vinegar
- 3 tablespoons chopped assorted fresh herbs (such as dill, basil, and mint)

- 6 cups fresh arugula leaves or small watercress sprigs
- 1 cup crumbled feta cheese (about 5 ounces)
- ½ cup sliced almonds, lightly toasted

Combine melon and tomatoes in large bowl. Sprinkle with 1 teaspoon fleur de sel and toss to blend; let stand 15 minutes. Add 4 tablespoons oil, vinegar, and herbs to melon mixture. Season to taste with pepper and more salt, if desired.

Toss arugula in medium bowl with remaining 1 tablespoon oil. Divide arugula among plates. Top with melon salad; sprinkle with feta cheese and toasted almonds and serve.

6 TO 8 SERVINGS

Spring Greens with Orange-Fennel Vinaigrette

¼ cup fresh blood-orange juice or fresh orange juice
2 tablespoons minced shallots
1 tablespoon fresh thyme leaves
2 teaspoons (packed) grated orange peel
1 teaspoon honey
½ cup extra-virgin olive oil
¼ cup finely chopped fresh fennel bulb
2 tablespoons chopped fennel fronds

3 blood oranges or seedless oranges
12 cups torn assorted salad greens (such as arugula, watercress, mâche, and endive) or 1½ five-ounce bags mixed baby greens
1 cup chopped green onions
⅔ cup walnuts, toasted

Whisk orange juice, shallots, thyme, orange peel, and honey in medium bowl to blend. Gradually whisk in oil, then fennel bulb and fennel fronds. Season dressing to taste with salt and pepper. *(Can be made 1 day ahead. Cover and chill. Rewhisk before using.)*

Cut all peel and white pith from oranges. Working over bowl, cut between membranes to release orange segments. Combine assorted greens, green onions, and toasted walnuts in large bowl. Drain orange segments and add to salad. Toss salad with enough dressing to coat evenly. Season to taste with salt and pepper and serve.

8 SERVINGS

Olive and Parmesan Skillet Cornbread

1¼ cups all purpose flour
 1 cup stone-ground yellow cornmeal
 1 tablespoon sugar
 1 tablespoon baking powder
 ½ teaspoon salt
 1 large egg
 2 teaspoons tomato paste
1½ teaspoons finely chopped fresh rosemary
 ½ teaspoon hot pepper sauce
 ¼ cup plus 1 tablespoon extra-virgin olive oil
 1 cup whole milk
 1 cup grated Parmesan cheese
 ½ cup pitted Kalamata olives, coarsely chopped

Preheat oven to 450°F. Place 9- to 10-inch cast-iron skillet or 9-inch-diameter ovenproof skillet (do not use nonstick) on center rack in oven. Heat for 30 minutes.

Whisk first 5 ingredients in large bowl. Whisk egg and next 3 ingredients in medium bowl to blend. Whisk ¼ cup oil, then milk into egg mixture. Add egg mixture to dry ingredients; stir batter just to blend. Stir in cheese and olives.

Remove skillet from oven. Add remaining 1 tablespoon oil to skillet; swirl to coat bottom and sides. Spoon batter into hot skillet. Place skillet in oven; reduce temperature to 400°F. Bake bread until golden and toothpick inserted into center comes out clean, about 22 minutes. Cool 5 minutes, then invert bread onto rack. Turn bread over. Serve warm or at room temperature.

8 SERVINGS

Herb Cheese Flatbread with Zucchini and Red Onion

Nonstick vegetable oil spray
 1 10-ounce tube refrigerated pizza dough
 ¾ cup garlic-and-herb cheese spread (such as Alouette), divided
 ¾ cup finely grated Parmesan cheese, divided
 3 tablespoons chopped fresh Italian parsley, divided
 1 small red onion
 1 7- to 8-inch-long zucchini (yellow or green), cut crosswise into ⅛-inch-thick rounds, divided
Olive oil

Preheat oven to 400°F. Line baking sheet with parchment; spray with nonstick spray. Unroll dough onto parchment. Spread half of herb cheese over 1 long half of dough, leaving ½-

inch plain border. Sprinkle with half of Parmesan and 2 tablespoons parsley. Using parchment as aid, fold plain half of dough over filled half (do not seal). Spread remaining herb cheese over; sprinkle with remaining Parmesan. Remove enough outer layers of onion to yield 2-inch-diameter core; cut into $1/8$-inch-thick rounds. Arrange 1 row of zucchini down 1 long side of dough. Arrange onion in row alongside zucchini. Arrange 1 more row of zucchini alongside onion. Brush vegetables with oil; sprinkle with salt and pepper. Bake bread until deep brown at edges, about 24 minutes. Top with 1 tablespoon parsley.

4 TO 6 SERVINGS

Brown Butter Soda Bread

¼ cup (½ stick) unsalted butter

3½ cups all purpose flour
½ cup old-fashioned oats
1 tablespoon sugar
1 tablespoon chopped fresh rosemary
2 teaspoons baking powder
1 teaspoon baking soda
1 teaspoon salt
¾ teaspoon ground black pepper plus additional for topping
1¾ cups buttermilk

1 egg white, beaten to blend

You'll get the most tender soda bread by kneading the dough gently and briefly, just until it comes together, so the gluten is minimally developed. The addition of rosemary and black pepper make this bread anything but typical. Wedges are delicious with plenty of butter and your favorite preserves.

Position rack in center of oven and preheat to 375°F. Stir butter in heavy small saucepan over medium heat until melted and golden brown, about 3 minutes. Remove from heat.

Stir flour, oats, sugar, rosemary, baking powder, baking soda, salt, and ¾ teaspoon pepper in large bowl to blend. Pour buttermilk and melted browned butter over flour mixture; stir with fork until flour mixture is moistened.

Turn dough out onto floured work surface. Knead gently until dough comes together, about 7 turns. Divide in half. Shape each half into ball; flatten each into 6-inch round. Place rounds on ungreased baking sheet, spacing 5 inches apart. Brush tops with beaten egg white. Sprinkle lightly with ground black pepper. Using small sharp knife, cut ½-inch-deep X in top of each dough round.

Bake breads until deep golden brown and tester inserted into center comes out clean, about 45 minutes. Cool breads on rack at least 30 minutes. Serve warm or at room temperature.

MAKES 2 LOAVES

Lavender Honey Tea Bread

- ½ cup whole milk
- 2 tablespoons lavender honey*
- 1 tablespoon plus ½ teaspoon dried lavender blossoms*

- 2½ cups all purpose flour
- 1 tablespoon baking powder
- ½ teaspoon baking soda
- ½ teaspoon salt

- 1 8-ounce container sour cream (1 cup)
- 1 cup sugar
- ½ cup (1 stick) unsalted butter, room temperature
- 3 large eggs

- 2 tablespoons powdered sugar

Bring milk to simmer in small saucepan; add honey and 1 tablespoon lavender blossoms. Stir until honey dissolves. Remove from heat; cover and let steep 30 minutes.

Meanwhile, preheat oven to 350°F. Butter and flour decorative 10-cup fluted pan or Bundt pan. Whisk flour, baking powder, baking soda, and salt in medium bowl.

Strain milk mixture into another medium bowl; discard solids in strainer. Whisk sour cream into milk mixture to blend. Using electric mixer, beat 1 cup sugar and butter in large bowl until light and fluffy. Add eggs 1 at a time, beating until blended after each addition. Add flour mixture alternately with milk mixture in 3 additions each, beating just until smooth. Transfer batter to prepared pan; smooth top of batter with rubber spatula.

Bake bread until tester inserted near center comes out clean, about 45 minutes. Cool bread in pan on rack 10 minutes. Turn bread out onto rack and cool completely.

Combine powdered sugar and remaining ½ teaspoon lavender blossoms in strainer set over small bowl. Press sugar mixture through strainer, discarding large bits. (*Can be made 1 day ahead. Cover and store at room temperature.*) Sift strained powdered sugar mixture over bread.

Lavender honey is available at specialty foods stores; dried lavender blossoms, also called culinary lavender buds, are available at natural foods stores, at farmers' markets, and by mail order.

8 TO 10 SERVINGS

Multi-Grain Bread

3	cups warm water (105°F to 115°F), divided
1½	cups (7 to 8 ounces) 7-grain cereal mix*
¾	cup (packed) golden brown sugar
3	envelopes active dry yeast
5	teaspoons salt
2	cups whole wheat flour
4½	cups (about) white all purpose flour
	Vegetable oil

Place 1 cup warm water in medium bowl. Stir in cereal mix; let stand 15 minutes.

Place remaining 2 cups warm water and sugar in large bowl. Stir in yeast. Let stand until yeast dissolves and mixture is foamy, about 7 minutes. Using sturdy rubber spatula, stir in cereal mixture and salt, then whole wheat flour and 4 cups white flour, 1 cup at a time. Knead in bowl until dough comes together. Knead on floured surface until smooth and elastic, sprinkling with white flour if very sticky, about 10 minutes (dough will be slightly sticky).

Oil clean large bowl. Add dough and turn to coat. Cover with plastic wrap and towel. Let rise in warm draft-free area until doubled in volume, about 1 hour 15 minutes. Punch down dough; divide into 3 pieces. Shape each into compact 4-inch-diameter ball. Sprinkle 2 heavy baking sheets with flour. Place 2 dough balls on 1 sheet and 1 dough ball on second sheet. Cover and let rise until doubled in volume, about 50 minutes.

Position 1 rack in bottom third and 1 rack in top third of oven; preheat to 375°F. Spray breads with water. Bake 25 minutes, spraying occasionally. Reverse sheets and bake until golden brown, spraying twice, about 30 minutes longer. Transfer breads to rack and cool.

Available at some supermarkets and natural foods stores.

MAKES 3 LOAVES

Brunch Buffet for 10

Scrambled Eggs

Bacon

Cantaloupe Salad with
Lime, Mint, and Ginger
(*double recipe; page 151*)

Lavender Honey Tea Bread
(*opposite; pictured opposite*)

Raspberry-Topped
Lemon Muffins
(*page 161*)

Mini Star-Anise Scones
(*page 162*)

Butter and Assorted Preserves

Orange Juice

Coffee and *Tea*

Mango Gingerbread with Macadamia Streusel

STREUSEL

⅓ cup finely chopped lightly salted dry-roasted macadamia nuts

¼ cup sugar

2½ tablespoons finely chopped crystallized ginger

GINGERBREAD

2 cups all purpose flour

¾ cup (packed) golden brown sugar

1½ tablespoons ground ginger

2 teaspoons baking powder

1 teaspoon baking soda

¼ teaspoon salt

1 pound ripe mangoes, peeled, pitted

½ cup buttermilk

¼ cup canola oil

2 large eggs

FOR STREUSEL: Stir all ingredients in small bowl to blend.

FOR GINGERBREAD: Position rack in center of oven and preheat to 350°F. Butter 9x9x2-inch metal baking pan. Whisk first 6 ingredients in medium bowl to blend. Coarsely puree

mangoes in food processor. Transfer 1 cup mango puree to large bowl (reserve any remaining puree for another use). Add buttermilk, oil, and eggs to puree; whisk until blended. Add flour mixture; stir just until combined. Transfer half of batter (about 2 cups) to prepared pan. Sprinkle half of streusel over. Spoon remaining batter over, smooth evenly with spatula, then sprinkle with remaining streusel.

Bake bread until springy to touch and tester inserted into center comes out clean, about 45 minutes. Cool completely in pan on rack. (*Can be made 8 hours ahead. Cover and store at room temperature.*) Cut bread into 9 squares and serve.

9 SERVINGS

Australian crystallized ginger is especially moist; it's sold at some supermarkets and specialty foods stores. Buttermilk and baking soda help give the gingerbread a tender texture.

Raspberry-Topped Lemon Muffins

1¼ cups sugar, divided
4 teaspoons finely grated lemon peel
2 cups all purpose flour
2½ teaspoons baking powder
¾ teaspoon salt
½ cup (1 stick) unsalted butter, room temperature
1 large egg
1 cup buttermilk
2 teaspoons vanilla extract

1½ ½-pint containers (about) fresh raspberries
¼ cup (about) whipping cream

Lemon sugar and fresh berries make these muffins special.

Preheat oven to 375°F. Line 14 standard muffin cups with paper liners. Mash ¼ cup sugar and lemon peel in small bowl until sugar is slightly moist. Whisk flour, baking powder, and salt in medium bowl to blend. Using electric mixer, beat remaining 1 cup sugar and butter in large bowl until smooth. Beat in egg. Beat in buttermilk, then vanilla and half of lemon sugar. Beat in flour mixture.

Divide batter among muffin cups. Top each muffin with 4 raspberries. Bake muffins until lightly browned on top and tester inserted into center comes out clean, about 35 minutes. Brush tops of muffins lightly with cream; sprinkle with remaining lemon sugar and cool.

MAKES 14

Three-Cheese Garlic Bread

- 2 tablespoons mayonnaise
- 2 tablespoons (¼ stick) butter, room temperature
- 1 garlic clove, pressed
- 1⅓ cups crumbled feta cheese
- 1¼ cups (about) grated Parmesan cheese, divided (about 4 ounces)
- ½ cup (packed) grated Monterey Jack cheese
- ½ cup finely chopped green onions
- 12 ¾-inch-thick slices pain rustique or ciabatta bread

Position rack in center of oven and preheat to 475°F. Mix first 3 ingredients in medium bowl. Mix in feta, ½ cup Parmesan, Jack cheese, and onions. Spread 2 tablespoons cheese mixture onto each bread slice. Top each with 1 tablespoon Parmesan; press to adhere. Place on baking sheet. Sprinkle lightly with salt and pepper. Bake until cheese is golden and bubbly, about 12 minutes.

MAKES 12 SLICES

Mini Star-Anise Scones

- ⅔ cup (about) heavy whipping cream, divided
- 1 large egg
- 2 teaspoons finely grated lemon peel
- 2¼ cups cake flour
- 3½ tablespoons sugar
- 1 tablespoon baking powder
- 2 teaspoons freshly ground star anise
- ½ teaspoon baking soda
- ½ teaspoon coarse kosher salt
- 6 tablespoons (¾ stick) chilled unsalted butter
- ½ cup raisins

- 2 tablespoons heavy whipping cream
- 2 tablespoons raw sugar*

Preheat oven to 400°F. Whisk ½ cup whipping cream, egg, and grated lemon peel in medium bowl. Whisk flour and next 5 ingredients in large bowl. Using large holes of box grater, grate butter over dry ingredients. Using fingertips, blend until coarse meal forms. Add raisins and cream mixture. Stir until moist clumps form, adding more cream by tablespoonfuls if dough is dry. Turn dough out onto floured surface; knead just until dough comes together.

Pat out dough to $\frac{1}{2}$-inch-thick round. Using 2-inch-diameter cutter, cut out scones. Gather dough scraps; press out to $\frac{1}{2}$-inch thickness and cut out additional scones. Transfer to baking sheet.

Brush tops of scones with 2 tablespoons whipping cream; sprinkle with raw sugar. Bake until golden and tester inserted into center comes out clean, about 16 minutes. Transfer to rack; cool. Serve scones warm or at room temperature.

Also called turbinado or demerara sugar; available at most supermarkets and at natural foods stores.

MAKES ABOUT 24

Get the freshest ground star anise by making your own. It's as easy as grinding a few star anise pods in a spice mill or a coffee grinder.

Cornmeal Biscuits with Cheddar and Chipotle

1	tablespoon unsalted butter
¾	cup (packed) chopped green onions
1½	cups all purpose flour
½	cup yellow cornmeal
2	tablespoons sugar
2½	teaspoons baking powder
¾	teaspoon coarse kosher salt
½	teaspoon baking soda
½	cup (1 stick) chilled unsalted butter, cut into ½-inch cubes
1½	cups (packed) coarsely grated yellow extra-sharp cheddar cheese
1	large egg
¾	cup (about) buttermilk
1	tablespoon finely minced canned chipotle chiles in adobo*
1	egg, beaten with 1 tablespoon whipping cream (for glaze)

Just follow these tips for biscuits that bake up perfectly every time:
- Use chilled butter; it will distribute more evenly throughout the biscuit dough.
- Don't substitute regular milk for the buttermilk: Slightly acidic, buttermilk adds tang and makes biscuits tender.
- Don't overwork the dough. For a light, fluffy biscuit, be sure to mix all of the ingredients together just until the dough is moist, and knead the dough gently just until it holds together.

Position rack in center of oven; preheat to 425°F. Melt 1 tablespoon butter in nonstick skillet over medium heat. Add green onions and sauté 2 minutes to soften slightly. Remove from heat.

Blend flour, cornmeal, sugar, baking powder, salt, and baking soda in processor. Add ½ cup chilled butter; cut in using on/off turns until mixture resembles coarse meal. Add cheese; cut in using on/off turns. Transfer flour mixture to large bowl. Whisk 1 egg in glass measuring cup. Add enough buttermilk to egg to measure 1 cup; stir in green-onion mixture and chipotles. Make well in center of dry ingredients. Pour buttermilk mixture into well; mix just until evenly moistened.

Turn dough out onto generously floured surface. Knead gently just until dough holds together, about 10 turns. Pat out on generously floured surface to ¾-inch-thick round. Using 3-inch round cutter, cut out biscuits. Transfer to ungreased baking sheet, spacing 1 inch apart. Gather dough scraps; pat out to ¾-inch thickness and cut out additional biscuits. Brush biscuits with egg glaze.

Bake biscuits until golden, tester inserted into center comes out clean, and biscuits feel firm, about 18 minutes. Cool on rack 5 minutes. Serve warm.

Available at some supermarkets, specialty foods stores, and Latin markets.

MAKES ABOUT 10

Strawberry-Topped Lemon Cupcakes
with Limoncello Glaze (page 199)

Desserts

Pies & Tarts

Fruit Desserts

Cakes

Mousses & Puddings

Frozen Desserts

Cookies & Pastries

Apple and Dried-Cherry Galette with Rich Caramel Sauce

CRUST

1½   cups all purpose flour
 ½   teaspoon salt
 ½   cup (1 stick) chilled unsalted butter, cut into ½-inch cubes
  3   tablespoons (or more) ice water

APPLE FILLING

  1   tablespoon unsalted butter
1½   to 1¾ pounds tart green apples (such as Granny Smith or Pippin), peeled, cored, each cut into 8 wedges
  5   tablespoons sugar, divided
 ⅓   cup dried tart cherries or cranberries
 ¼   teaspoon ground cinnamon

Chilled crème fraîche
Rich Caramel Sauce (see recipe)

FOR CRUST: Blend flour and salt in processor. Add butter; using on/off turns, cut in until coarse meal forms. Add 3 tablespoons ice water. Blend until moist clumps form, adding more water by teaspoonfuls if dough is dry. Gather into ball; flatten into disk. Wrap and chill at least 30 minutes and up to 1 day.

FOR APPLE FILLING: Melt butter in large nonstick skillet over medium heat. Add apples; sprinkle with 3 tablespoons sugar. Sauté until apples are golden and beginning to soften, about 20 minutes. Stir in cherries and cinnamon. Cool.

Preheat oven to 375°F. Roll out dough on lightly floured parchment paper to 12-inch round. Transfer parchment with dough to rimless baking sheet. Arrange apple filling in center 6 inches of dough, leaving 3-inch plain border. Fold border over filling, pleating gently and pinching together any cracks in dough to seal. Sprinkle filling and dough border with 2 tablespoons sugar.

Bake galette until crust is golden and apples are tender, about 40 minutes. Cool galette 15 minutes on sheet. Slide long knife under galette to loosen from parchment; slide onto platter. Serve with crème fraîche and caramel sauce.

6 SERVINGS

Rich Caramel Sauce

- 1½ cups sugar
- ½ cup water
- 3 tablespoons unsalted butter
- 1 cup heavy whipping cream

Stir sugar and water in heavy large saucepan over medium-low heat until sugar dissolves, occasionally brushing down sides of pan with wet pastry brush. Increase heat; boil without stirring until syrup is deep amber, swirling pan occasionally, about 12 minutes. Remove pan from heat. Whisk in butter. Gradually pour in cream (mixture will bubble up). Return pan to low heat; stir until sauce is smooth. Pour into bowl. Cool to lukewarm. (*Can be made 2 days ahead. Cover and chill. Rewarm before using.*)

MAKES ABOUT 2 CUPS

French Country Menu for 6

Pâté, Cornichons, and
Sliced Baguette

Mustard-Roasted Chicken
(*page 72*)

Spring Vegetable Fricassee with
Saffron Cream
(*double recipe; page 132*)

Roasted Potatoes

Chablis

Apple and Dried-Cherry Galette
with Rich Caramel Sauce
(*opposite; pictured opposite*)

Caramelized-Banana Tartlets with Bittersweet Chocolate-Port Sauce

CRUST

½ cup (1 stick) unsalted butter, room temperature

½ cup powdered sugar

½ cup hazelnuts, lightly toasted, ground

1 teaspoon finely grated orange peel

½ teaspoon vanilla extract

½ teaspoon salt

1 cup all purpose flour

FILLING

4 tablespoons (½ stick) unsalted butter, divided

6 medium-size slightly under-ripe bananas, peeled, each cut on diagonal into ½-inch-thick slices, divided

½ cup sugar, divided

6 tablespoons warm water, divided

1 pint premium vanilla ice cream

Bittersweet Chocolate-Port Sauce (see recipe)

FOR CRUST: Using electric mixer, beat first 6 ingredients in medium bowl to blend. Add flour; beat until moist clumps form. Gather dough into ball; flatten into disk. Wrap in plastic; chill 30 minutes.

Preheat oven to 350°F. Divide dough into 6 equal pieces. Press 1 piece evenly onto bottom and up sides of each of six 4½-inch-diameter tartlet pans with removable bottoms. Bake crusts until deep golden brown and cooked through, about 25 minutes. Cool crusts completely in pans on rack. (*Can be prepared 1 day ahead. Cover and store at room temperature.*)

FOR FILLING: Melt 2 tablespoons butter in large nonstick skillet over medium-high heat until beginning to brown. Add half of bananas to skillet in single layer; cook until bananas brown on bottom, about 45 seconds. Using thin spatula, turn slices over; sprinkle ¼ cup sugar evenly over bananas. Cook until sugar dissolves and turns golden, occasionally swirling pan, about 3 minutes. Turn banana slices over; add 3 tablespoons warm water and continue cooking until caramel thickens slightly, swirling pan, about 2 minutes. Arrange banana slices in each of 3 tartlet crusts; spoon any caramel from skillet over. Clean skillet, then repeat procedure with remaining butter, bananas, sugar, and water. (*Can be prepared 2 hours ahead. Let stand uncovered at room temperature. Warm in 350°F oven 10 minutes before continuing recipe.*)

Top each tartlet with scoop of vanilla ice cream. Drizzle each tartlet with Bittersweet Chocolate-Port Sauce and serve.

MAKES 6

Bittersweet Chocolate-Port Sauce

- ¾ cup whipping cream
- ¼ cup whole milk
- ¼ cup (½ stick) unsalted butter
- 8 ounces bittersweet or semisweet chocolate, chopped
- ¼ cup tawny Port

These tartlets use a crust that's especially easy to make: It gets pressed into the pan, rather than rolled out.

Bring whipping cream, whole milk, and unsalted butter to simmer in small heavy saucepan. Remove saucepan from heat and add chopped chocolate. Whisk mixture until smooth. Stir in tawny Port. (*Sauce can be made 2 days ahead. Cover and chill. Warm over medium-low heat.*)

MAKES ABOUT 2 CUPS

Lemon Cloud Tart with Rhubarb Compote

LEMON CURD FILLING

- 4 large egg yolks
- 3 large eggs
- ½ cup fresh lemon juice
- ½ cup (1 stick) unsalted butter, diced
- ½ cup sugar

HAZELNUT CRUST

- ½ cup hazelnuts, toasted
- ½ cup (1 stick) unsalted butter, room temperature
- ⅓ cup powdered sugar
- 1 tablespoon (packed) finely grated lemon peel
- 1 large egg yolk
- 1¼ cups all purpose flour
- ¼ teaspoon fine sea salt

LEMON CRÈME FRAÎCHE

- ¾ cup chilled heavy whipping cream
- ¾ cup crème fraîche
- 3 tablespoons sugar
- 1 tablespoon finely grated lemon peel
  Rhubarb Compote (see recipe)

FOR LEMON CURD FILLING: Whisk yolks and eggs in medium bowl to blend. Combine lemon juice, butter, and ½ cup sugar in large metal bowl. Set bowl over saucepan of simmering water; whisk until butter melts and sugar dissolves. Gradually whisk ⅓ of hot butter mixture into eggs, then whisk mixture back into bowl with remaining butter mixture. Whisk constantly over simmering water until custard thickens and thermometer inserted into mixture registers 180°F, about 5 minutes (do not boil). Pour lemon curd through

strainer set over another medium bowl. Place plastic wrap directly on surface of lemon curd; chill overnight. (*Can be made 2 days ahead. Keep refrigerated.*)

FOR HAZELNUT CRUST: Finely grind hazelnuts in processor. Using electric mixer, beat butter, powdered sugar, and lemon peel in medium bowl until well blended. Add yolk and beat until smooth. Beat in hazelnuts, then flour and salt. Gather dough into ball; flatten into disk. Wrap dough in plastic and chill 1 hour.

Preheat oven to 350°F. Roll dough out on floured surface to 12-inch round. Transfer to 9-inch-diameter tart pan with removable bottom. Press crust onto bottom and up sides of pan; trim dough overhang. Chill 20 minutes. Bake crust until golden brown and cooked through, pressing with fork if crust bubbles, about 25 minutes. Cool crust in pan on rack. (*Can be prepared 1 day ahead. Cover and store at room temperature.*)

FOR LEMON CRÈME FRAÎCHE: Using electric mixer, beat whipping cream, crème fraîche, 3 tablespoons sugar, and lemon peel in large bowl until stiff peaks form. Spoon half of lemon curd and half of lemon crème fraîche into another large bowl. Using small rubber spatula, gently fold lemon curd and lemon crème fraîche together, creating marble effect and being careful not to overmix to retain marbling. Spoon marbled mixture in dollops into cooled crust. Using tip of knife or small rubber spatula, swirl and pull mixture upward in peaks. Repeat with remaining curd and crème fraîche mixture. Refrigerate tart at least 1 hour and up to 4 hours. Remove pan sides. Place tart on platter. Serve with Rhubarb Compote.

8 SERVINGS

A filling of lemon curd folded into whipped crème fraîche gives this tart its billowy texture. At the market, look for thin, reddish pink stalks of rhubarb—they'll give the most colorful, tender, and flavorful results. And be sure to avoid using the leaves, which are toxic.

Rhubarb Compote

    4 cups ½-inch pieces fresh rhubarb (from about 1½ pounds)
1½ cups sugar
    2 tablespoons fresh lemon juice

Combine all ingredients in heavy large saucepan. Stir over medium heat until sugar dissolves. Reduce heat to medium-low, cover, and simmer until rhubarb is just tender, stirring occasionally, about 7 minutes. Transfer rhubarb mixture to bowl. Cover and chill until cold, about 2 hours. (*Can be made 1 day ahead. Keep refrigerated.*)

MAKES ABOUT 3 CUPS

Milky Way Tartlets

CRUST

¾ cup plus 2 tablespoons all purpose flour

2 tablespoons plus 2 teaspoons unsweetened cocoa powder (preferably Dutch process)

½ cup (1 stick) unsalted butter, room temperature

½ cup plus 2 tablespoons powdered sugar

1 large egg yolk

FILLING

3½ ounces high-quality milk chocolate (such as Lindt or Perugina), chopped

2 cups heavy whipping cream, divided

¼ cup (½ stick) unsalted butter

½ cup plus 2 tablespoons sugar

3 tablespoons water

Unsweetened cocoa powder (for dusting)

FOR CRUST: Whisk flour and cocoa in medium bowl. Beat butter and powdered sugar in another bowl until well blended. Beat in yolk. Add flour mixture in 2 additions, beating just until blended. Gather dough into ball; flatten into disk. Wrap in plastic; chill 2 hours.

Divide dough into 6 equal pieces. Press each onto bottom and up sides of 4½-inch-diameter tartlet pan with removable bottom. Refrigerate crusts 1 hour or freeze 30 minutes.

Preheat oven to 375°F. Bake cold crusts until set and dry-looking, about 12 minutes, pressing with back of spoon if bubbles form. Cool crusts in pans. *(Can be made 1 day ahead. Cover; store at room temperature.)*

FOR FILLING: Place milk chocolate in medium bowl. Bring 1½ cups cream to simmer in small saucepan. Pour hot cream over chocolate; let stand 1 minute, then whisk until melted and smooth. Cover with plastic wrap and refrigerate until cold, at least 4 hours or overnight.

Combine ½ cup cream and butter in small saucepan and stir over medium heat until butter melts; remove from heat. Combine sugar and 3 tablespoons water in heavy small saucepan. Stir over medium-low heat until sugar dissolves. Increase heat; boil without stirring until color is deep amber, occasionally brushing down sides of pan with wet pastry brush and swirling pan, about 8 minutes. Immediately add hot cream mixture (mixture will bubble vigorously). Remove from heat and stir until any caramel bits dissolve. Transfer caramel to small bowl and chill until slightly firm, stirring often, about 40 minutes.

Spoon caramel into center of crusts (about 2 generous tablespoons for each). Set aside.

Using electric mixer, beat chilled milk chocolate-cream mixture until peaks form; spoon atop caramel in crusts, dividing equally (about ½ cup for each crust) and spreading evenly. Chill at least 2 hours. *(Can be made 8 hours ahead. Cover and keep refrigerated.)*

Remove tartlets from pans. Lightly sift cocoa powder over tartlets and serve.

MAKES 6

Key Lime Pie with Passion Fruit Coulis and Huckleberry Compote

COMPOTE

16 ounces fresh wild huckleberries or wild Maine blueberries or one 15- to 16-ounce package frozen wild blueberries

½ cup sugar

1 vanilla bean, split lengthwise

COULIS

¾ cup frozen passion fruit puree,* thawed

½ cup sugar

½ vanilla bean, split lengthwise

CRUST

1¼ cups graham cracker crumbs

3 tablespoons sugar

Pinch of salt

6 tablespoons (¾ stick) unsalted butter, melted

FILLING

1 14-ounce can sweetened condensed milk

4 large egg yolks

½ cup fresh Key lime juice or regular lime juice

Whipped cream

FOR COMPOTE: Combine huckleberries and sugar in medium saucepan. Scrape in seeds from vanilla bean; add bean. Bring to simmer over medium heat, stirring until sugar dissolves. Simmer until reduced to 1¼ cups, about 15 minutes. Refrigerate until cold. (*Can be made 2 days ahead. Cover and refrigerate. Discard vanilla bean before serving.*)

FOR COULIS: Combine passion fruit puree and sugar in heavy small saucepan. Scrape in seeds from vanilla bean; add bean. Stir over medium heat until sugar dissolves. Simmer until mixture is reduced to ½ cup, stirring frequently, about 6 minutes. Transfer coulis to bowl and refrigerate until cold. (*Can be made 2 days ahead. Cover and keep refrigerated. Discard vanilla bean before using.*)

FOR CRUST: Preheat oven to 350°F. Combine cracker crumbs, sugar, and salt in medium bowl. Add butter and stir until crumbs are moist. Press mixture onto bottom and up sides of 9-inch-diameter glass pie dish. Bake crust until set and lightly browned, about 10 minutes. Cool crust completely. Maintain oven temperature.

FOR FILLING: Whisk sweetened condensed milk and egg yolks in medium bowl to blend.

Add lime juice and whisk until blended. Pour filling into cooled crust. Bake pie until filling is set, about 18 minutes. Transfer to rack and cool to room temperature. Cover and refrigerate pie overnight.

Cut pie into wedges. Spoon huckleberry compote on top. Garnish with whipped cream. Drizzle passion fruit coulis around and serve.

Available at some specialty foods stores.

8 SERVINGS

Almond, Apricot, and Cream Cheese Crostata

½ 7-ounce log almond paste
3½ tablespoons sugar, divided
3 ounces cream cheese, cut into ½-inch cubes
1 large egg yolk
1 teaspoon vanilla extract
1 refrigerated pie crust (half of 15-ounce package), room temperature
5 to 6 large apricots, quartered, pitted
¼ cup apricot jam, heated

3 crushed amaretti cookies (Italian macaroons)*

Preheat oven to 400°F. Blend almond paste and 3 tablespoons sugar in processor until finely chopped. Add cream cheese, egg yolk, and vanilla and blend until filling is smooth. Unroll crust on heavy rimmed baking sheet. Spread filling over crust, leaving 1½-inch plain border. Arrange apricot quarters, rounded side down, in spoke pattern in 2 concentric circles atop filling. Fold dough border up over edge of filling. Brush exposed apricots with warm jam. Sprinkle with remaining 1½ teaspoons sugar.

Bake crostata until crust is golden brown and apricots are tender and slightly browned, about 43 minutes. Sprinkle with crushed amaretti. Cool 30 minutes. Serve warm or at room temperature.

Available at some supermarkets and Italian markets.

8 SERVINGS

Chocolate, Caramel, and Walnut Tart

CRUST

1½ cups all purpose flour

¼ teaspoon salt

½ cup (1 stick) chilled unsalted butter, cut into ½-inch cubes

4 tablespoons (or more) ice water

FILLING

1 cup sugar (preferably baker's sugar or other superfine sugar)

¼ cup water

1 cup heavy whipping cream

¼ cup (½ stick) unsalted butter, room temperature

2 tablespoons honey

2 teaspoons vanilla extract

2 ounces bittersweet (not unsweetened) or semisweet chocolate, chopped

2 ounces semisweet chocolate, chopped

2½ cups (about 9 ounces) walnuts, toasted, cut into ½-inch pieces

Vanilla ice cream

FOR CRUST: Blend flour and salt in processor 5 seconds. Add butter to processor. Using on/off turns, blend until coarse meal forms. Add 4 tablespoons ice water. Blend until dough just begins to come together, adding more ice water by teaspoonfuls if dry. Gather dough; flatten into disk. Wrap; chill at least 1 hour.

Roll out dough on lightly floured surface to 14-inch round. Transfer to 11-inch-diameter tart pan with removable bottom. Cut off all but ½ inch of overhang. Fold overhang in and press, forming double-thick sides. Pierce crust all over with fork; chill 30 minutes.

Preheat oven to 400°F. Line crust with foil; fill with dried beans or pie weights. Bake 20 minutes. Remove foil and beans. Bake until golden, pressing with back of fork if crust bubbles, about 20 minutes longer. Cool completely.

FOR FILLING: Stir 1 cup sugar and ¼ cup water in heavy large saucepan over low heat until sugar dissolves. Increase heat. Bring to boil, brushing down sides of pan with wet pastry brush. Boil without stirring until deep amber color, swirling pan occasionally, about 8 minutes. Remove from heat; add cream (mixture will bubble up). Return pan to low heat; whisk caramel until smooth. Add butter, honey, and vanilla. Whisk until sauce thickens slightly, about 3 minutes. Remove from heat. Add all chocolate; whisk until smooth. Stir in nuts. Spread filling in crust. Chill tart until firm, at least 3 hours or overnight.

Serve with vanilla ice cream.

10 TO 12 SERVINGS

Peach and Blackberry Shortcakes with Blackberry Cream

SHORTCAKES

2⅓ cups all purpose flour

8 tablespoons sugar, divided

2½ teaspoons baking powder

½ teaspoon fine sea salt

¼ teaspoon ground nutmeg

10 tablespoons (1¼ sticks) chilled unsalted butter, cut into ½-inch cubes

¾ cup plus 2 tablespoons buttermilk

1 tablespoon whipping cream

FILLING

2 pounds ripe peaches, peeled, pitted, sliced

2 6-ounce containers blackberries

⅓ cup sugar

Pinch of fine sea salt

BLACKBERRY CREAM

2 6-ounce containers blackberries

¾ cup sugar

1¾ cups chilled whipping cream

1 teaspoon vanilla extract

FOR SHORTCAKES: Position rack in center of oven and preheat to 400°F. Line rimmed baking sheet with parchment paper. Whisk flour, 7 tablespoons sugar, baking powder, salt, and nutmeg in large bowl to blend. Add butter and rub in with fingertips until mixture resembles coarse meal. Gradually add buttermilk, tossing with fork until moist clumps form. Gather dough together; flatten dough on floured work surface to ¾- to 1-inch-thick round. Using floured 3-inch round biscuit cutter or cookie cutter, cut out rounds. Gather dough scraps and flatten on work surface to ¾- to 1-inch thickness; cut out additional rounds for a total of 6. Transfer shortcakes to prepared baking sheet. Whisk cream and remaining 1 tablespoon sugar in small bowl to blend. Brush cream mixture over tops of shortcakes.

Bake shortcakes until tops begin to brown and tester inserted into center comes out clean, about 25 minutes. Transfer shortcakes to rack. (*Can be made 6 hours ahead. Let stand at room temperature. Rewarm in 350°F oven 5 minutes before assembling.*)

FOR FILLING: Toss sliced peaches, blackberries, sugar, and salt in medium bowl; let stand while preparing blackberry cream.

FOR BLACKBERRY CREAM: Rinse blackberries; moisture will enhance puree. Place in processor. Add sugar; puree until smooth. Strain mixture through fine strainer set over bowl, pressing on solids to extract as much liquid as possible. Discard solids.

Using electric mixer, beat cream and vanilla in large bowl until peaks form. Fold ¾ cup blackberry puree into whipped cream until incorporated. Reserve remaining blackberry puree for sauce.

Cut shortcakes horizontally in half. Place 1 bottom half of each shortcake on each of 6 plates. Spoon filling over each, then generous amount of blackberry cream. Drizzle each with reserved blackberry puree. Cover with top halves of shortcakes and serve.

MAKES 6

Spiced Blueberry Grunt

FILLING

4 cups fresh blueberries (from four ½-pint containers)

½ cup (packed) golden brown sugar

¼ cup mild-flavored (light) molasses

¼ cup water

3 tablespoons fresh lemon juice

2 teaspoons finely grated lemon peel

¼ teaspoon ground nutmeg

¼ teaspoon ground cloves

DUMPLINGS

1½ cups all purpose flour

2 tablespoons sugar

2 teaspoons baking powder

¾ teaspoon fine sea salt

3 tablespoons chilled unsalted butter, cut into ¼-inch cubes

¾ cup whole milk

Whipped cream, chilled whipping cream, or vanilla ice cream

FOR FILLING: Mix all ingredients in 12-inch-diameter skillet. Bring to boil over medium-high heat, stirring until sugar dissolves. Reduce heat to medium; simmer until berries soften and mixture thickens slightly, about 10 minutes.

MEANWHILE, PREPARE DUMPLINGS: Whisk flour, sugar, baking powder, and salt in medium bowl to blend. Add butter and rub in with fingertips until mixture resembles fine meal. Add milk; stir just until blended and sticky dough forms.

Drop batter by tablespoonfuls onto simmering berry mixture, placing close together. Reduce heat to medium-low; cover skillet and simmer until dumplings are firm and tester inserted into dumplings comes out clean, about 25 minutes.

Scoop warm dessert into bowls. Top with whipped cream, whipping cream, or vanilla ice cream.

6 TO 8 SERVINGS

Grunts get their quirky name from the fact that the fruit, which is topped with dumplings and cooked on the stove in a covered skillet, can make a grunting sound as the dessert steams. Molasses adds sweetness and a lovely depth of flavor to this version of the dessert.

Warm Baby Bananas with Dulce de Leche Sauce

1   9- to 10-ounce jar dulce de leche or caramel sauce
¾   cup dulce de leche liqueur*
2   tablespoons fresh lemon juice
2   teaspoons sugar
½   teaspoon ground cinnamon
     Large pinch of ground nutmeg
12 baby bananas, peeled

2   tablespoons (¼ stick) unsalted butter
     Crushed amaretti cookies or almond macaroons**

Baby bananas are sweeter than regular bananas. Choose ones that are ripe but firm.

Whisk dulce de leche sauce and liqueur in small saucepan over low heat until sauce is just warm. Whisk lemon juice, sugar, cinnamon, and nutmeg in large bowl to blend; add bananas and toss to coat.

Melt butter in large skillet over medium-high heat. Add bananas; sauté until heated through and beginning to brown, turning gently with heat-resistant rubber spatula, about 5 minutes. Transfer 2 bananas to each of 6 plates. Drizzle warm sauce over. Sprinkle with crushed amaretti and serve.

Available at some supermarkets, liquor stores, and Latin markets.
**Available at some supermarkets and Italian markets.*

6 SERVINGS

Pear and Dried-Cherry Custard Crisp

TOPPING

- ¾ cup all purpose flour
- 6 tablespoons (packed) golden brown sugar
- ¼ cup pecans, ground in processor
- 1 teaspoon ground cinnamon
- 1 teaspoon finely grated lemon peel
- ½ teaspoon salt
- ½ cup (1 stick) unsalted butter, melted
- 1 teaspoon vanilla extract

CUSTARD

- 2 large eggs
- 1 cup crème fraîche
- 1 teaspoon vanilla extract
- 1 tablespoon all purpose flour

FILLING

- 3½ pounds firm but ripe Bosc pears, peeled, cored, cut into 1½-inch chunks (about 8 cups)
- 1 cup dried tart cherries (about 6 ounces)
- 2 tablespoons fresh lemon juice
- ⅓ cup all purpose flour
- ½ cup baker's sugar (superfine sugar) or regular sugar
- 2½ teaspoons finely grated lemon peel

French vanilla ice cream

FOR TOPPING: Mix first 6 ingredients in medium bowl. Add melted butter and vanilla extract; stir with fork until soft crumbly dough forms. (*Can be made up to 6 hours ahead. Cover; let stand at room temperature.*)

FOR CUSTARD: Whisk eggs in medium bowl to blend. Whisk in crème fraîche and vanilla. Sift in flour; whisk until smooth. (*Can be made up to 6 hours ahead. Cover and chill; rewhisk before using.*)

FOR FILLING: Preheat oven to 375°F. Generously butter 13x9x2-inch oval ceramic or glass baking dish. Combine pears, cherries, and lemon juice in large bowl; toss to blend. Mix flour, sugar, and lemon peel in small bowl. Add to pear mixture and toss to blend. Transfer pear mixture to prepared dish, pressing slightly with rubber spatula to form even layer. (*Can be made up to 1 hour ahead; let stand at room temperature.*)

Pour custard evenly over pear mixture. Using fingertips, crumble topping evenly over. Bake until pears are tender and topping is deep golden, about 55 minutes. Remove from oven and let stand 10 minutes. Serve warm or at room temperature with ice cream.

8 SERVINGS

Skillet Blackberry Cobbler

CRUST

- 3 cups all purpose flour
- ¾ cup sugar
- 1½ teaspoons baking powder
- ¾ teaspoon salt
- ¾ cup chilled solid vegetable shortening, cut into 1-inch pieces
- 3 tablespoons chilled unsalted butter, cut into ½-inch cubes
- 4 tablespoons (or more) ice water

STREUSEL

- 1 cup all purpose flour
- ½ cup sugar
- 1 teaspoon ground cinnamon
- ¼ teaspoon salt
- ½ cup (1 stick) chilled unsalted butter, cut into ½-inch cubes

FILLING

- 2 cups sugar
- 1½ cups all purpose flour
- ¼ teaspoon salt
- 1½ cups sour cream
- 6 large eggs
- 7 cups fresh blackberries

  Vanilla ice cream

FOR CRUST: Blend flour, sugar, baking powder, and salt in processor. Add shortening and butter. Blend until coarse meal forms. Add 4 tablespoons ice water. Using on/off turns, blend until moist clumps form, adding more water by teaspoonfuls if dry. Gather dough into ball; flatten into disk. Wrap and chill at least 30 minutes and up to 1 day.

FOR STREUSEL: Blend first 4 ingredients in processor 5 seconds. Add butter. Using on/off turns, blend until crumbly mixture forms. Transfer to bowl. Cover and chill.

FOR FILLING: Preheat oven to 350°F. Whisk 2 cups sugar, flour, and salt in medium bowl. Whisk sour cream and eggs in large bowl. Stir dry ingredients into sour cream mixture. Fold in fresh blackberries.

Press crust dough over bottom and up sides (but not on top edge) of 12-inch-diameter cast-iron skillet or casserole with 2½-inch-high sides (about 15-cup capacity). Spoon in filling. Sprinkle with streusel.

Bake until top is golden and center is cooked through and puffed, about 1½ hours. Cool 30 minutes. Serve warm or at room temperature. Serve with ice cream.

12 SERVINGS

Grilled Brown-Sugar Peaches with White Chocolate

4 tablespoons (½ stick) unsalted butter, melted
2 tablespoons (packed) dark brown sugar
½ teaspoon ground cinnamon
4 unpeeled peaches, halved, pitted
⅓ cup finely chopped white chocolate
3 tablespoons coarsely chopped toasted salted pistachios

For a twist, drizzle amaretto or balsamic vinegar over the grilled peaches just before serving.

Prepare barbecue (medium-high heat). Whisk first 3 ingredients in large bowl to blend. Add peach halves; toss to coat well. Place peaches, cut side down, on grill. Grill until slightly charred, about 1 minute. Using tongs, turn peaches over. Divide chopped white chocolate among peach cavities and drizzle remaining butter mixture from bowl over chocolate. Grill until chocolate just begins to melt and peaches are charred, about 2 minutes. Divide peach halves among bowls. Sprinkle with pistachios and serve.

4 SERVINGS

Deep Dark Chocolate Cheesecake

CRUST

24 chocolate wafer cookies (from one 9-ounce package)
1 tablespoon sugar
¼ cup (½ stick) butter, melted

FILLING

1 9.7-ounce bar Scharffen Berger 70% Cacao Bittersweet Chocolate,* chopped
4 8-ounce packages cream cheese, room temperature
1¼ cups plus 2 tablespoons sugar
¼ cup unsweetened cocoa powder (preferably Scharffen Berger)
4 large eggs

TOPPING

¾ cup whipping cream
6 ounces Scharffen Berger 70% Cacao Bittersweet Chocolate,* chopped
1 tablespoon sugar

Bittersweet chocolate curls

FOR CRUST: Preheat oven to 350°F. Butter 9-inch-diameter springform pan with 3-inch-high sides. Blend cookies in processor until finely ground; blend in sugar. Add melted butter and process until well blended. Press cookie crumbs evenly onto bottom (not sides) of prepared pan. Bake just until set, about 5 minutes. Cool cookie crust while preparing filling. Maintain oven temperature.

FOR FILLING: Stir chopped chocolate in metal bowl set over saucepan of simmering water until melted and smooth. Remove bowl from over water; cool chocolate until lukewarm but still pourable. Blend cream cheese, sugar, and cocoa powder in processor until smooth. Blend in eggs 1 at a time. Mix in lukewarm chocolate. Pour filling over crust; smooth top. Bake until center is just set and just appears dry, about 1 hour. Cool 5 minutes. Run knife around sides of cake to loosen. Chill overnight.

FOR TOPPING: Stir cream, 6 ounces chocolate, and sugar in heavy medium saucepan over low heat until smooth. Cool slightly. Pour over center of cheesecake, spreading to within ½ inch of edge and filling any cracks. Chill until topping is set, about 1 hour. (*Can be made 3 days ahead. Cover with foil and keep refrigerated.*)

CAKES

Release pan sides. Transfer cheesecake to platter. Top with chocolate curls. Let stand 2 hours at room temperature before serving.

If unavailable, substitute another high-quality bittersweet chocolate.

12 SERVINGS

Banana Layer Cake with Caramel Cream and Pecans

CAKE

2½ cups all purpose flour

1 tablespoon baking powder

½ teaspoon (generous) fine sea salt

¾ cup (1½ sticks) unsalted butter, room temperature

2½ cups sugar, divided

6 large eggs

1 cup plus 2 tablespoons buttermilk

2 small ripe bananas, peeled, cut into ¼-inch cubes (about 1½ cups)

BANANA-CARAMEL CREAM

1½ cups (packed) golden brown sugar

1 small ripe banana, peeled, cut into 1-inch pieces

3 tablespoons unsalted butter, room temperature

3¾ cups chilled heavy whipping cream, divided

4½ teaspoons fresh lime juice, divided

4½ teaspoons dark rum, divided

Sea Salt-Roasted Pecans (see recipe)

FOR CAKE: Preheat oven to 350°F. Butter and flour two 9-inch-diameter cake pans with 1½-inch-high sides. Sift flour, baking powder, and sea salt into medium bowl. Beat butter and 1 cup sugar in large bowl until well blended. Add 2 eggs; beat until blended. Add dry ingredients to butter mixture in 4 additions alternately with buttermilk in 3 additions. Beat remaining 4 eggs and remaining 1½ cups sugar in medium bowl until mixture is thick and pale in color, about 4 minutes. Fold egg mixture into batter. Fold in bananas. Divide batter between prepared pans (about 3½ cups for each).

Bake cakes until tester inserted into center comes out clean, about 35 minutes. Transfer to rack; cool 15 minutes. Invert cakes onto racks; cool completely. (*Can be made 1 day ahead. Wrap in foil; store at room temperature.*)

FOR BANANA-CARAMEL CREAM: Combine brown sugar, banana, and 3 tablespoons butter in processor; blend until smooth. Add 1½ cups whipping cream; blend. Transfer to heavy medium saucepan. Whisk over medium heat until sugar dissolves and mixture boils. Attach candy thermometer to inside of pan; cook without stirring or swirling pan until temperature registers 218°F, about 10 minutes. Pour caramel into bowl. Cool to room temperature, whisking occasionally.

Whisk remaining 2¼ cups whipping cream in large bowl until cream mounds softly. Gradually fold in cool caramel mixture. Chill until firm enough to spread, about 3 hours.

Cut each cake horizontally into 2 layers. Place 1 layer, cut side up, on platter. Drizzle 1½ teaspoons lime juice and 1½ teaspoons rum over. Spread 1¼ cups banana cream over.

Top with second cake layer. Drizzle 1½ teaspoons lime juice and 1½ teaspoons rum over. Spread 1½ cups cream over. Repeat with third cake layer, lime juice, rum, and banana cream. Top with fourth cake layer, cut side down; spread remaining cream over top.

Scatter roasted pecans over top of cake. *(Can be made 1 day ahead. Cover with cake dome and refrigerate.)*

10 TO 12 SERVINGS

The salty-sweet contrast is terrific, especially in a layer cake with a creamy banana and caramel filling and salty roasted pecans.

Sea Salt-Roasted Pecans

    2 cups pecan halves
    3 tablespoons unsalted butter, melted
  1¼ teaspoons fine sea salt

Preheat oven to 325°F. Toss pecans and butter in medium bowl to coat. Add salt and toss. Spread pecans in single layer on rimmed baking sheet.

Bake until fragrant and slightly darkened in color, about 15 minutes. Cool pecans on baking sheet. *(Can be made 2 days ahead. Store airtight at room temperature. Before using, rewarm in 350°F oven for 5 minutes, then cool.)*

MAKES 2 CUPS

Almond-Plum Buckle

Nonstick vegetable oil spray

½ cup whole almonds (about 2½ ounces)
1½ cups all purpose flour
1 teaspoon baking powder
¼ teaspoon fine sea salt
1 cup (2 sticks) unsalted butter, room temperature
1 cup plus 4 teaspoons sugar
2 large eggs
1 teaspoon vanilla extract
½ teaspoon almond extract

1¼ pounds plums (about 8 medium), halved, pitted, cut into ½-inch-thick slices
¾ teaspoon ground cinnamon

Position rack in center of oven and preheat to 350°F. Spray 9-inch-diameter cake pan with 2-inch-high sides with nonstick spray. Line bottom of pan with parchment paper round.

Finely grind almonds in processor. Transfer to medium bowl; whisk in flour, baking powder, and salt. Using electric mixer, beat butter in large bowl until fluffy. Add 1 cup sugar; beat until well blended. Add eggs 1 at a time, beating well after each addition. Beat in vanilla and almond extracts, then flour mixture just until incorporated.

Transfer batter to prepared pan; spread evenly and smooth top with spatula. Gently press plum slices, flesh side down, into batter in spoke pattern around outer rim and center of cake, placing close together. Mix cinnamon and 4 teaspoons sugar in small bowl. Sprinkle cinnamon-sugar over plums.

Bake cake until tester inserted into center comes out clean, about 50 minutes. Cool cake in pan on rack 20 minutes. Run small knife between cake and pan sides to loosen. Invert cake onto platter; remove parchment paper. Place another platter atop cake. Using both hands, hold both platters firmly together and invert cake, plum side up. Cool cake completely. Cut into wedges.

8 SERVINGS

Spiced Coconut Loaf Cake

1¼ cups all purpose flour
2 teaspoons baking powder
1 teaspoon ground allspice
1 teaspoon ground cinnamon
½ teaspoon ground nutmeg
¼ teaspoon salt
½ cup canned cream of coconut (such as Coco López)
½ cup sour cream

¾ cup (packed) dark brown sugar
½ cup (1 stick) unsalted butter, room temperature
2 large eggs
½ cup sweetened flaked coconut plus more for garnish

Powdered sugar

Preheat oven to 350°F. Butter 9x5x3-inch metal loaf pan. Line pan bottom with parchment paper. Whisk first 6 ingredients in medium bowl. Whisk cream of coconut and sour cream in small bowl.

Using electric mixer, beat brown sugar and butter in large bowl until smooth. Beat in eggs 1 at a time. Beat in flour mixture in 3 additions alternately with sour cream mixture in 2 additions. Stir in ½ cup coconut. Transfer batter to prepared pan.

Bake cake until tester inserted into center comes out clean, about 45 minutes. Cool 5 minutes. Turn out onto rack; peel off paper. Cool.

Place cake on platter. Sift powdered sugar over; sprinkle with coconut and serve.

10 TO 12 SERVINGS

Buckles are aptly named: Fruit is baked along with a layer of cake batter that rises to the top, buckling as it cooks. Vanilla ice cream or lightly sweetened whipped cream is great with this.

Upside-Down Butterscotch Apple Sour Cream Cake

CAKE
- 1½ cups all purpose flour
- 1½ teaspoons baking powder
- ¾ teaspoon salt
- ½ cup (1 stick) unsalted butter, room temperature
- ⅔ cup baker's sugar (superfine sugar) or regular sugar
- 2 large eggs
- 1½ teaspoons vanilla extract
- ½ cup sour cream
- ½ Golden Delicious apple, peeled, cored, finely chopped (about ¾ cup)

BUTTERSCOTCH-CARAMEL APPLES
- 6 tablespoons (¾ stick) unsalted butter
- ⅓ cup (packed) dark brown sugar
- ⅓ cup butterscotch morsels
- 2 8-ounce Golden Delicious apples, peeled, halved, cored, cut into ¼-inch-thick slices

FOR CAKE: Preheat oven to 375°F. Mix flour, baking powder, and salt in medium bowl. Using electric mixer, beat butter in large bowl until smooth. Gradually add sugar and beat until well blended. Add eggs and vanilla; beat until blended. Beat in flour mixture, then sour cream. Stir in chopped apple. Set aside while preparing butterscotch-caramel apples.

FOR BUTTERSCOTCH-CARAMEL APPLES: Melt butter in 10-inch-diameter nonstick oven-proof skillet over medium heat. Add brown sugar and butterscotch morsels; stir until melted and smooth and mixture is bubbling, about 2 minutes. Add apple slices to skillet and cook until golden brown, using tongs to turn slices, about 3 minutes per side (there will be a lot of liquid in skillet). Remove skillet from heat and let cool 3 minutes. Using tongs, arrange apple slices in skillet in concentric circles or other pattern.

Carefully spoon cake batter in small dollops atop apples in skillet. Using offset spatula, gently spread batter evenly to edges of skillet (batter will seem to float on top of apples and pan juices). Bake until cake is golden brown and tester inserted into center comes out clean, about 30 minutes. Cool in skillet 10 minutes. Run knife around edges of cake to loosen. Place large platter atop skillet. Using oven mitts or pot holders, hold platter and skillet firmly together and invert, allowing cake to settle onto platter. Serve cake warm.

8 SERVINGS

Semisweet Chocolate Layer Cake
with Vanilla Cream Filling

CAKE

6 ounces semisweet chocolate, chopped

¾ cup all purpose flour
¾ cup cake flour
½ teaspoon baking powder
½ teaspoon baking soda
½ teaspoon coarse kosher salt
1¾ cups (packed) dark brown sugar
6 tablespoons (¾ stick) unsalted butter, room temperature
1 teaspoon vanilla extract
2 large eggs
¾ cup buttermilk

CREAM FILLING

1 teaspoon unflavored gelatin

1½ cups chilled whipping cream, divided

¼ cup powdered sugar
½ teaspoon vanilla extract

GANACHE

1 cup heavy whipping cream
⅔ cup light corn syrup
18 ounces semisweet chocolate, chopped

Additional powdered sugar

FOR CAKE: Preheat oven to 325°F. Butter three 8-inch-diameter cake pans with 1½-inch-high sides. Line bottoms with parchment paper round; butter parchment. Place chocolate in metal bowl set over saucepan of simmering water. Stir until melted and smooth.

Whisk all purpose flour and next 4 ingredients in medium bowl. Using electric mixer, beat brown sugar, butter, and vanilla in large bowl to blend (mixture will be crumbly). Add eggs 1 at a time, beating well after each addition. Beat in warm melted chocolate. Mix in dry ingredients in 2 additions alternately with buttermilk in 1 addition. Divide batter among prepared pans.

Bake cakes until tester inserted into center comes out clean, about 23 minutes. Cool cakes in pans 10 minutes. Turn cakes out onto rack; peel off parchment. Cool cakes completely. *(Can be made 1 day ahead. Wrap cakes in plastic and store at room temperature.)*

FOR CREAM FILLING: Place 2 tablespoons cold water in small bowl. Sprinkle unflavored gelatin over; let stand 10 minutes to soften.

Bring $^1/_2$ cup cream to boil in heavy small saucepan. Add cream to softened gelatin; stir until dissolved. Place in refrigerator just until cold, whisking frequently, about 5 minutes.

Place remaining 1 cup chilled cream, powdered sugar, and vanilla extract in medium bowl. Using electric mixer, beat until peaks form. Add gelatin mixture and beat until peaks form.

Place 1 cake on 8-inch cardboard round or tart pan bottom. Spread half of filling over. Top with second cake. Spread remaining filling over. Top with third cake. Chill on cardboard round 3 hours.

FOR GANACHE: Bring whipping cream and corn syrup to simmer in heavy small saucepan. Remove from heat. Add chopped chocolate and whisk until ganache is smooth. Cool.

Place cake on rack set in large rimmed baking sheet. Spread half of ganache over top and sides of cake. Chill cake 1 hour. Rewarm remaining ganache in small saucepan over low heat just until luke-warm, whisking often. Pour ganache over cold cake, spreading as needed to cover top and sides. Chill until ganache is set, about 1 hour. (*Can be made 1 day ahead. Keep chilled.*)

Cut out paper heart shapes of differing sizes and arrange atop cake. Sift powdered sugar over. Carefully lift hearts from cake and serve.

10 TO 12 SERVINGS

Peach and Mascarpone Cheesecake with Balsamic Syrup

CRUST

7 whole graham crackers, broken into pieces

⅓ cup sugar

5 tablespoons unsalted butter, diced

FILLING

3 8-ounce packages mascarpone cheese

1 cup sugar

3 tablespoons all purpose flour

3 large eggs

½ teaspoon vanilla extract

2 large peaches (about 1 pound), peeled, pitted, diced

½ cup balsamic vinegar

½ cup sliced peaches

FOR CRUST: Preheat oven to 350°F. Blend graham cracker pieces, sugar, and butter in processor until moist clumps form. Press onto bottom (not sides) of 9-inch-diameter springform pan. Bake until golden brown, about 12 minutes. Transfer crust to rack to cool. Maintain oven temperature.

FOR FILLING: Using electric mixer, beat mascarpone, sugar, and flour in large bowl until blended. Beat in eggs 1 at a time; add vanilla extract. Puree diced peaches in mini processor or blender until smooth. Beat puree into batter. Pour filling into crust. Bake until edges are raised and dry and center is softly set, about 1 hour 5 minutes. Place hot cheesecake directly in refrigerator. Chill uncovered overnight.

Boil balsamic vinegar in small saucepan until reduced to ¼ cup, about 4 minutes; cool syrup. Cut around cheesecake; remove pan sides. Top with peach slices, drizzle with balsamic vinegar syrup, and serve.

10 SERVINGS

Strawberry-Topped Lemon Cupcakes with Limoncello Glaze

CUPCAKES
- 2 cups cake flour
- 1½ teaspoons baking powder
- ½ teaspoon salt
- 1½ cups sugar
- ½ cup (1 stick) unsalted butter, room temperature
- 4 large eggs
- ¾ cup buttermilk
- ½ cup fresh lemon juice
- ¼ cup finely grated lemon peel

GLAZE AND TOPPING
- ¾ cup (or more) powdered sugar
- 3 tablespoons unsalted butter
- 3 tablespoons limoncello or other lemon liqueur
- 3 tablespoons fresh lemon juice
- 1½ teaspoons finely grated lemon peel

- 18 strawberries

FOR CUPCAKES: Preheat oven to 350°F. Line 18 standard muffin cups with paper liners. Sift flour, baking powder, and salt into medium bowl. Using electric mixer, beat sugar and butter in large bowl until fluffy. Beat in eggs 1 at a time. Beat in dry ingredients in 3 additions alternately with buttermilk in 2 additions. Beat in lemon juice and lemon peel. Divide batter among liners.

Bake cupcakes until tester inserted into center comes out clean, about 18 minutes. Transfer cupcakes to racks.

MEANWHILE, PREPARE GLAZE AND TOPPING: Stir ¾ cup powdered sugar, butter, limoncello, lemon juice, and grated lemon peel in small saucepan over low heat until butter melts and glaze comes to simmer. Whisk in additional powdered sugar by tablespoonfuls if glaze is very thin. Spoon 1 teaspoon warm glaze over each warm cupcake. Cool cupcakes completely.

Arrange 1 strawberry atop each cupcake. Drizzle remaining limoncello glaze over. Let cupcakes stand until glaze sets, about 2 hours. (*Can be prepared 1 day ahead. Cover and let stand at room temperature.*)

MAKES 18

Dessert Buffet for 18

Champagne

Chocolate, Caramel, and Walnut Tart
(*double recipe; page 178*)

Banana Layer Cake with Caramel Cream and Pecans
(*page 190*)

Strawberry-Topped Lemon Cupcakes with Limoncello Glaze
(*at left*)

Soft Ginger Cookies
(*page 227*)

Milk Chocolate-Peanut Butter Sandwich Cookies
(*page 228*)

Pumpkin Cheesecake Crumble Squares
(*page 233*)

Chocolate-Dipped Strawberries

Coffee and *Tea*

Chocolate-Mint Pudding Cakes

6 ounces bittersweet (not unsweetened) or semisweet chocolate, chopped
½ cup (1 stick) unsalted butter, cut into 4 pieces

3 large eggs
3 large egg yolks
⅓ cup baker's sugar (superfine sugar) or regular sugar
¼ cup all purpose flour
1¼ teaspoons peppermint extract
¼ teaspoon salt

Powdered sugar or sweetened cocoa powder
Peppermint stick ice cream or mint chocolate chip ice cream
Fresh mint leaves

To avoid overbaking the pudding cakes, start checking early for doneness.

Preheat oven to 375°F. Lightly butter six ¾-cup ramekins or custard cups. Stir chocolate and butter in heavy small saucepan over low heat until melted and smooth. Remove from heat and cool slightly.

Using electric mixer, beat eggs, egg yolks, and ⅓ cup sugar in large bowl until slightly thickened, about 5 minutes. Add all purpose flour and beat until blended. Add chocolate mixture, peppermint extract, and salt; beat just until incorporated. Divide chocolate mixture among prepared ramekins. Place ramekins on baking sheet. (*Can be prepared 1 hour ahead. Let stand at room temperature.*)

Bake cakes until edges are set but centers look shiny and still move slightly when ramekins are gently shaken (tester inserted into centers comes out with wet batter attached), about 11 minutes. Remove cakes from oven; run small knife around each cake to loosen.

Place small plate atop 1 ramekin with pudding cake. Using oven mitts or pot holders, hold plate and ramekin firmly together and invert, allowing cake to settle onto plate. Repeat with remaining cakes. Sprinkle each cake with powdered sugar or sweetened cocoa. Place scoop of ice cream alongside. Garnish with mint leaves and serve.

MAKES 6

Rum Cake with Rum Raisin Ice Cream and Island Fruit

CAKE

- 3 cups all purpose flour
- 2½ teaspoons baking powder
- 1¼ cups (2½ sticks) unsalted butter, room temperature
- 1¾ cups sugar
- ½ teaspoon salt
- 5 large eggs
- 1 cup water
- 1 teaspoon vanilla extract

SAUCE

- 1 cup (packed) golden brown sugar
- ½ cup heavy whipping cream
- ¼ cup (½ stick) unsalted butter, cut into ½-inch cubes
- 3 tablespoons dark rum
- 2 tablespoons dark corn syrup
- ¾ teaspoon ground allspice
- ¼ teaspoon ground nutmeg

  Rum raisin ice cream
- 4 cups chopped tropical fruit (such as pineapple, mango, papaya, and guava)
  Toasted chopped pecans

FOR CAKE: Preheat oven to 350°F. Butter 9-inch-diameter springform pan with 3-inch-high sides. Whisk flour and baking powder in medium bowl. Beat butter, sugar, and salt in large bowl until light and fluffy, about 4 minutes. Add eggs 1 at a time, beating well after each addition. Mix 1 cup water and vanilla extract in measuring cup. Fold flour mixture into butter mixture in 3 additions alternately with water mixture in 2 additions. Transfer batter to prepared springform pan.

Bake cake until tester inserted into center comes out clean, about 1 hour 10 minutes. Cool completely in pan on rack. (*Can be made 1 day ahead. Store airtight at room temperature.*)

FOR SAUCE: Combine first 7 ingredients in heavy medium saucepan. Stir over medium heat until sugar dissolves, about 3 minutes. Increase heat to medium-high. Boil without stirring until sauce is reduced to 1½ cups, about 5 minutes. Cool slightly. (*Can be prepared 1 day ahead. Let stand at room temperature. Rewarm slightly before continuing.*)

Remove sides from cake pan. Slice cake. Place 1 wedge on each plate. Place scoop of ice cream alongside. Spoon chopped tropical fruit alongside. Drizzle cake with sauce. Sprinkle with chopped pecans and serve.

12 SERVINGS

Dark Chocolate Soufflés with Cardamom Crème Anglaise

5 ounces bittersweet chocolate, chopped
1 tablespoon unsalted butter
¼ cup plus 3 tablespoons sugar
2 tablespoons all purpose flour
1 teaspoon unsweetened cocoa powder
¾ cup whole milk
¼ teaspoon vanilla extract
4 large egg yolks

5 large egg whites
¼ teaspoon coarse kosher salt

Cardamom Crème Anglaise (see recipe)

Place chocolate and butter in medium bowl. Whisk ¼ cup sugar, flour, and cocoa powder in small bowl. Bring milk and vanilla to boil in heavy small saucepan. Gradually whisk hot milk mixture into sugar mixture to blend. Return mixture to same saucepan. Cook over medium-high heat until thick paste forms, stirring constantly, about 2 minutes. Scrape mixture into bowl with chocolate and butter; stir until chocolate is melted (mixture may look curdled). Add egg yolks and whisk until mixture looks shiny and creamy. (*Soufflé base can be prepared 1 day ahead. Press plastic wrap directly onto surface and refrigerate. Bring soufflé base to room temperature before continuing.*)

Butter eight ¾-cup soufflé dishes or custard cups; dust with sugar. Using electric mixer, beat egg whites until frothy. With mixer running, gradually add 3 tablespoons sugar, then salt; beat just until soft peaks form. Fold ⅓ of whites into soufflé base until well combined. Gently fold in remaining egg whites just to blend (some white streaks may remain). Divide batter among prepared dishes. Place on rimmed baking sheet. (*Can be made 2 hours ahead. Let stand at room temperature.*)

Preheat oven to 350°F. Bake soufflés until puffed above rim of dish, tops are flat, and edges are set, about 12 minutes. Serve immediately with Cardamom Crème Anglaise.

MAKES 8

Cardamom Crème Anglaise

- 2 tablespoons whole green cardamom pods, crushed
- 1 cup whole milk
- 1 cup whipping cream
- ½ cup sugar, divided
- ¼ vanilla bean, split lengthwise
- 4 large egg yolks

Place cardamom pods with seeds in heavy medium saucepan over medium-high heat. Stir until pods brown, about 5 minutes. Add milk, cream, and ¼ cup sugar. Scrape seeds from vanilla bean into pan; add bean. Bring mixture to boil. Whisk egg yolks and remaining ¼ cup sugar in medium bowl. Gradually whisk in hot milk mixture. Return mixture to same saucepan. Stir over medium-low heat until custard thickens and leaves path on back of spoon when finger is drawn across, stirring constantly, about 2 minutes (do not boil). Cover and chill until cold, about 3 hours. Strain into medium pitcher. (*Can be made 2 days ahead. Cover and refrigerate.*)

MAKES 2 CUPS

Crème anglaise is both a classic custard sauce and the base for many ice creams. Make a double batch and process half in an ice cream maker for a frozen treat. To crack cardamom pods without losing the tiny seeds, crush them in a mortar with a pestle, or place the pods in a resealable plastic bag, then crush with a rolling pin or meat tenderizer.

Sticky Date and Almond Bread Pudding with Amaretto Zabaglione

8 cups 1½-inch cubes egg bread with crust (from one 16-ounce loaf)

2¼ cups chopped pitted Medjool dates (about 12 ounces)

½ cup sliced almonds

6 large eggs

2 large egg yolks

1 cup baker's sugar (superfine sugar) or regular sugar

3½ cups half and half

1 tablespoon vanilla extract

¼ teaspoon (generous) ground nutmeg

Powdered sugar
Amaretto Zabaglione (see recipe)

Arrange bread cubes in single layer on rimmed baking sheet. Let stand at room temperature to dry overnight.

Butter 13x9x2-inch glass baking dish. Transfer bread to prepared dish. Mix dates and almonds in medium bowl. Sprinkle over bread and toss to distribute evenly. Using electric mixer, beat eggs and egg yolks in large bowl until frothy. Add 1 cup sugar and beat until mixture thickens and is pale yellow, about 5 minutes. Add half and half, vanilla, and nutmeg; beat just until blended. *(Bread mixture and custard can be prepared 2 hours ahead. Let bread mixture stand uncovered at room temperature. Chill custard; rewhisk before continuing.)*

Preheat oven to 375°F. Pour custard over bread mixture, then press lightly on bread with rubber spatula to submerge. Let stand 15 minutes, occasionally pressing lightly on bread.

Bake bread pudding 25 minutes. Using large spoon, press bread down, allowing custard in dish to rise to surface. Spoon custard evenly over bread mixture. Continue to bake pudding until knife inserted into center of custard comes out clean, about 20 minutes longer.

Remove bread pudding from oven and let stand 10 minutes. Sprinkle with powdered sugar. Serve warm with warm or chilled Amaretto Zabaglione.

10 TO 12 SERVINGS

Amaretto Zabaglione

6 large egg yolks

⅓ cup amaretto or other almond liqueur

3 tablespoons baker's sugar (superfine sugar) or regular sugar

¼ cup whipping cream

Whisk egg yolks, amaretto, and sugar in medium metal bowl to blend. Set bowl over saucepan of simmering water. Whisk mixture constantly and vigorously until thickened

and instant-read thermometer inserted into mixture registers 140°F for 3 minutes, about 5 minutes total. Remove mixture from over water. Add cream and whisk until incorporated. Serve warm or chilled. (*If serving chilled, zabaglione can be prepared 1 day ahead and refrigerated. Rewhisk before serving.*)

MAKES ABOUT 1²⁄₃ CUPS

Medjools are the most prized of all dates, and their firm, meaty texture is perfect for this recipe.

Chilled Lemon Soufflés with Caramel Sauce

Vegetable oil
¼ cup water
1 teaspoon unflavored gelatin

3 large eggs, separated
2 tablespoons cornstarch
1 cup plus 2 tablespoons whole milk
6 tablespoons sugar, divided
6 tablespoons fresh lemon juice
1½ teaspoons finely grated lemon peel

Caramel Sauce (see recipe)

Lightly oil six ³⁄₄-cup soufflé dishes or custard cups; set aside. Pour ¼ cup water into small bowl. Sprinkle gelatin over; let stand until gelatin softens, about 15 minutes.

Meanwhile, whisk egg yolks and cornstarch in medium bowl until smooth. Combine milk and 3 tablespoons sugar in heavy medium saucepan; stir over medium heat until sugar dissolves and mixture comes to simmer. Gradually whisk ¹⁄₃ of hot milk mixture into yolk mixture. Pour mixture back into remaining milk mixture in saucepan. Whisk constantly over medium-high heat until custard boils and thickens, about 2 minutes. Reduce heat to medium and whisk 2 minutes longer. Remove from heat; whisk in lemon juice and lemon peel. Add gelatin mixture; stir until gelatin dissolves. Transfer custard to medium bowl; let stand 10 minutes to cool slightly.

Whisk egg whites and remaining 3 tablespoons sugar in medium bowl to blend. Set bowl over saucepan of simmering water (do not allow bottom of bowl to touch water); whisk constantly until instant-read thermometer inserted into mixture registers 140°F, about 2 minutes. Transfer egg white mixture to large bowl of stand mixer and beat until stiff peaks form. Fold into warm lemon custard in 3 additions.

Divide lemon custard among prepared soufflé dishes; level off tops with back of knife. Refrigerate soufflés uncovered overnight. (*Can be prepared 2 days ahead. Cover and keep refrigerated.*)

Run small knife around soufflés to loosen. Place small plate atop 1 soufflé and invert. Using both hands, hold plate and soufflé dish tightly together and shake gently, allowing soufflé to settle on plate (if soufflé does not release from dish, place bottom of soufflé dish in 1 inch of warm water for 20 seconds). Repeat with remaining soufflés. Spoon room-temperature Caramel Sauce generously over top of each soufflé.

MAKES 6

Caramel Sauce

¾ cup sugar
½ cup water
¼ cup light corn syrup
¾ cup whipping cream

Combine sugar, ½ cup water, and corn syrup in heavy medium saucepan. Stir over medium heat until sugar dissolves. Increase heat and boil without stirring until mixture turns deep amber color, occasionally brushing down sides of pan with wet pastry brush and swirling pan, about 10 minutes. Remove from heat. Carefully add cream (you may want to stand back—mixture will bubble vigorously). Stir sauce over low heat until any caramel bits dissolve and sauce is smooth. (*Can be prepared 1 day ahead. Cover and refrigerate. Rewarm over medium-low heat just until pourable.*) Let Caramel Sauce cool to room temperature.

MAKES ABOUT 1⅓ CUPS

Silky caramel sauce poured over a light soufflé makes for an opulent textural contrast. And unlike a warm soufflé that you bake, this chilled version (and the sauce) can be made ahead.

Turkish Coffee Pudding

2¼ cups heavy whipping cream, divided
3 tablespoons Kahlúa or other coffee liqueur, divided
2 tablespoons instant espresso powder plus additional for garnish
1 teaspoon (scant) ground cardamom plus additional for garnish
4 large egg yolks
½ cup (packed) golden brown sugar

Combine 1¾ cups cream, 2 tablespoons Kahlúa, 2 tablespoons espresso powder, and 1 scant teaspoon cardamom in heavy small saucepan; bring to simmer. Whisk egg yolks and brown sugar in medium bowl. Gradually whisk hot cream mixture into yolk mixture; return to pan. Stir over medium-low heat until mixture is thick enough to coat back of spoon (do not boil), about 5 minutes. Strain through fine-mesh strainer into 2-cup measuring cup. Divide among 6 demitasse cups. Chill until set, about 5 hours. (*Can be made 1 day ahead. Keep chilled.*)

Whisk ½ cup cream in medium bowl until peaks form. Whisk in 1 tablespoon Kahlúa. Top each pudding with whipped cream. Sprinkle with additional espresso powder and additional cardamom.

6 SERVINGS

A bit of cardamom gives this dessert its exotic flavor. The pudding needs to chill about five hours before serving, so be sure to plan ahead.

Tangerine-Honey Flan with Grapefruit Segments

¾ cup sugar, divided
¼ cup water

2 large eggs
4 large egg yolks
1 tablespoon honey
1 teaspoon vanilla extract
  Pinch of salt
¾ cup heavy whipping cream
¼ cup sweetened condensed milk
¼ cup finely chopped tangerine peel (cut from 3 large tangerines with
    vegetable peeler)
1 cup fresh tangerine juice

2 pink grapefruits

Position rack in center of oven and preheat to 350°F. Bring ½ cup sugar and ¼ cup water to boil in heavy small saucepan over medium-low heat, stirring until sugar dissolves and brushing down sides of pan with wet pastry brush. Increase heat and boil without stirring until syrup is deep amber color, swirling pan occasionally, about 7 minutes. Pour caramel syrup into 8-inch-diameter cake pan with 1½-inch-high sides; quickly rotate pan so syrup covers bottom.

Whisk eggs, yolks, honey, vanilla, and salt in medium bowl to blend. Bring cream, condensed milk, and tangerine peel to simmer in medium saucepan. Slowly whisk hot cream mixture into egg mixture. Whisk in tangerine juice. Strain custard into caramel-lined pan. Place pan into 13x9x2-inch metal baking pan. Pour enough hot water into baking pan to come halfway up sides of cake pan.

Bake flan until set in center when cake pan is slightly moved, about 40 minutes. Remove from water; cool 30 minutes. Chill flan uncovered until very cold and firm, at least 6 hours. (*Can be made 1 day ahead. Cover; keep chilled.*)

Cut all peel and pith from grapefruits. Working over medium bowl, cut between membranes, releasing segments. Chill until ready to use.

Cut around flan in pan. Place plate on top of pan and invert, releasing flan. Cut into wedges; serve with grapefruit.

6 SERVINGS

Dinner and a Movie for 6

Spiced Nuts

Quinoa with Moroccan Winter Squash and Carrot Stew
(*page 106*)

Butter Lettuce Salad with Champagne Vinaigrette

Gewürztraminer

Tangerine-Honey Flan with Grapefruit Segments
(*at left; pictured opposite*)

Strawberry Tiramisù

1¼ cups strawberry preserves

⅓ cup plus 4 tablespoons Cointreau or other orange liqueur, divided

⅓ cup orange juice

1 pound mascarpone cheese,* room temperature

1⅓ cups chilled whipping cream

⅓ cup sugar

1 teaspoon vanilla extract

1½ pounds fresh strawberries, divided

52 (about) crisp ladyfingers (Boudoirs or Savoiardi)

Whisk preserves, ⅓ cup Cointreau, and orange juice in 2-cup measuring cup. Place mascarpone cheese and 2 tablespoons Cointreau in large bowl; fold just to blend. Using electric mixer, beat cream, sugar, vanilla, and remaining 2 tablespoons Cointreau in another large bowl to soft peaks. Stir ¼ of whipped cream mixture into mascarpone mixture to lighten. Fold in remaining whipped cream.

Hull and slice half of strawberries. Spread ½ cup preserve mixture over bottom of 3-quart oblong serving dish or 13x9x2-inch glass baking dish. Arrange enough ladyfingers over preserve mixture to cover bottom of dish. Spoon ¾ cup preserve mixture over ladyfingers, then spread 2½ cups mascarpone mixture over. Arrange sliced strawberries over mascarpone mixture. Repeat layering with remaining ladyfingers, preserve mixture, and mascarpone mixture. Cover with plastic and chill at least 8 hours or overnight.

Slice remaining strawberries. Arrange over tiramisù and serve.

An Italian cream cheese that's sold at supermarkets and Italian markets.

8 SERVINGS

Cherry-Almond Clafouti

½ cup whole almonds (about 2 ounces)

1¼ cups whole milk

1 tablespoon plus ½ cup sugar

8 ounces dark sweet cherries, pitted, halved (about 2 cups)

3 large eggs, room temperature

½ teaspoon almond extract

Pinch of salt

¼ cup all purpose flour

Powdered sugar

Clafouti is a rustic, simple French dessert that's a cross between a pancake and a custard. You can use other fruits, but cherries are traditional.

Blend almonds in processor until ground but not pasty. Transfer to small saucepan; add milk and bring to simmer. Remove from heat; let steep 30 minutes. Pour through fine strainer, pressing on solids to extract as much liquid as possible. Discard solids in strainer.

Preheat oven to 375°F. Butter 10-inch-diameter glass pie dish; sprinkle with 1 tablespoon sugar. Scatter cherries over bottom of dish.

Using electric mixer, beat eggs, almond extract, salt, and remaining ½ cup sugar in medium bowl until well blended. Add strained almond milk and beat to blend. Sift flour into egg mixture and beat until smooth. Pour mixture over cherries. Bake until set and knife inserted into center comes out clean, about 30 minutes. Cool completely. (*Can be made 6 hours ahead. Let stand at room temperature.*)

Lightly dust clafouti with powdered sugar and serve.

6 SERVINGS

Lime Marscapone Panna Cotta with Raspberries

      6 tablespoons fresh lime juice, divided
  1½ teaspoons grated lime peel
      1 teaspoon unflavored gelatin
  1¼ cups whipping cream, divided

   ½ cup mascarpone cheese or cream cheese
   ¾ cup sugar, divided

      1 tablespoon butter
  1½ 6-ounce containers raspberries (about 2 cups)
      1 lime

Combine ¼ cup juice and peel in small saucepan; sprinkle gelatin over. Let stand 5 minutes. Add ¼ cup cream to gelatin mixture; stir over low heat just until gelatin dissolves. Remove from heat.

Whisk mascarpone and ½ cup sugar in medium bowl; gradually whisk in remaining 1 cup cream until smooth. Whisk gelatin mixture into cream mixture. Pour into 6 widemouthed Champagne glasses or small wineglasses. Chill until set, at least 4 hours or overnight.

Stir remaining 2 tablespoons lime juice, ¼ cup sugar, and butter in large skillet over medium-high heat until sugar dissolves, about 3 minutes. Cool 2 minutes. Fold in berries; spoon over desserts. Grate peel from 1 lime directly over desserts.

6 SERVINGS

Thai Coconut Tapioca Pudding

      1 2x1-inch piece fresh ginger, peeled, sliced
      1 1x1-inch piece fresh galangal,* peeled, sliced
   10 Thai basil leaves*
      6 fresh cilantro sprigs
      2 kaffir lime leaves* or 2 teaspoons grated lime peel
      1 tablespoon sliced lemongrass*
      2 cups water

      2 cups whole milk
   ½ cup sugar
   ½ cup small pearl tapioca* (not quick-cooking)
      1 13.5- to 14-ounce can unsweetened coconut milk*

      1 large mango, peeled, cut into cubes
      1 tablespoon fresh lime juice
         Pinch of cayenne pepper
         Thai basil sprigs

Combine first 6 ingredients in food processor; blend 20 seconds. Transfer to medium saucepan; add 2 cups water and bring to boil. Remove pan from heat and let steep uncovered 20 minutes. Pour mixture into strainer set over heavy large saucepan; press on solids to release flavored liquid. Discard solids in strainer.

Add milk and sugar to flavored liquid in pan; bring to boil. Stir in tapioca; return to boil. Reduce heat to medium and simmer uncovered until pudding thickens and is reduced to 2¼ cups, stirring frequently, about 35 minutes. Stir in coconut milk (pudding will be runny). Transfer to bowl. Cover and refrigerate overnight.

Toss mango cubes, lime juice, and cayenne in medium bowl. Divide tapioca among 6 stemmed glasses or bowls. Top with mango mixture; garnish with basil sprigs.

Galangal, Thai basil, kaffir lime leaves, lemongrass, small pearl tapioca, and unsweetened coconut milk are available at Asian markets.

6 SERVINGS

Dinner from the Trattoria for 6

Bruschetta

Pasta with Eggplant, Basil, and Ricotta Salata
(page 113)

Radicchio Salad

Chianti

Lime Mascarpone Panna Cotta with Raspberries
(opposite)

Chocolate Meringue and Mint Chip Ice Cream Cake

10½ tablespoons sugar, divided

½ cup powdered sugar

3 tablespoons unsweetened cocoa powder

4 large egg whites

2 pints mint chip ice cream, slightly softened

½ cup chilled whipping cream

¼ teaspoon vanilla extract

¼ cup chocolate sprinkles

Position 1 rack in top third and 1 rack in bottom third of oven and preheat to 200°F. Line 2 large baking sheets with parchment paper. Trace two 12x4-inch rectangles, spaced slightly apart, on 1 paper. Trace one 12x4-inch rectangle on second paper. Turn papers over (marked lines should show through). Sift 3 tablespoons sugar, powdered sugar, and cocoa into medium bowl. Using electric mixer, beat egg whites in large bowl until frothy. Add 1½ tablespoons sugar and beat until soft peaks form. Gradually add 5 tablespoons sugar, beating until whites are stiff and glossy. Fold in cocoa mixture. Spread ⅓ of meringue (about 1½ cups) evenly over each marked rectangle. Bake meringues until dry, reversing sheets every hour, about 4 hours total. Turn off oven; leave meringues in oven overnight.

Lift meringues from parchment. Place 2 meringues on work surface. Gently spread 1 pint ice cream over each, being careful not to press hard to avoid cracking meringues. Place 1 filled meringue on long platter. Top with second filled meringue, then third meringue, pressing lightly to adhere. Cover and freeze assembled cake at least 2 hours and up to 1 day.

Beat cream, vanilla, and remaining 1 tablespoon sugar in small bowl until peaks form. Spread whipped cream on top layer of meringue to cover; scatter chocolate sprinkles evenly over. Cut crosswise into slices and serve.

8 TO 10 SERVINGS

Chocolate-Cinnamon Gelato with Toffee Bits

½ cup sugar

2 tablespoons cornstarch

1¼ teaspoons ground cinnamon

Pinch of salt

2 cups whole milk, divided

5 ounces bittersweet (not unsweetened) or semisweet chocolate, finely chopped

½ cup chilled heavy whipping cream

⅓ cup coarsely crushed toffee candy (such as Skor, Heath bar, or Almond Roca)

Whisk sugar, cornstarch, cinnamon, and salt in heavy medium saucepan until blended. Gradually add ¼ cup milk, whisking until cornstarch is dissolved. Whisk in remaining 1¾ cups milk. Whisk over medium-high heat until mixture thickens and comes to boil, about 6 minutes. Reduce heat to medium and cook 1 minute longer, whisking occasionally. Remove from heat; add chocolate. Let stand 1 minute, then whisk until melted and smooth.

Transfer gelato base to medium bowl. Mix in cream. Place bowl over large bowl filled with ice and water and cool, stirring often, about 30 minutes.

Process gelato base in ice cream maker according to manufacturer's instructions, adding toffee during last minute of churning. Transfer to container; cover. Freeze at least 3 hours and up to 2 days.

MAKES ABOUT 3 CUPS

Fresh Peach Ice Cream with Blackberries

 1 cup plus 2 tablespoons sugar
 3 large egg yolks
 1 cup heavy whipping cream
 1 cup whole milk
2½ cups mashed pitted very ripe unpeeled peaches (1½ pounds)
 3 tablespoons light corn syrup

    Fresh blackberries

Whisk sugar and egg yolks in medium bowl. Bring cream and milk to simmer in large saucepan; gradually whisk into yolk mixture. Return to same pan. Stir over medium-low heat until custard thickens enough to leave path on back of spoon when finger is drawn across, about 6 minutes (do not boil). Pour into large bowl; mix in peaches and corn syrup. Chill uncovered until cold, at least 1 hour.

Process custard in ice cream maker according to manufacturer's instructions. Transfer to container; cover. Freeze about 6 hours. Serve with blackberries. *(Can be prepared 2 days ahead. Keep frozen.)*

MAKES ABOUT 1½ QUARTS

This recipe was inspired by the ice cream Lady Bird Johnson made at the White House. (She loved Texas peaches so much that she had them shipped to Washington.) Because the peaches aren't peeled, rinse them well and rub dry to remove any fuzz.

Raspberry-Cassis Ice Cream

    1   12-ounce bag frozen unsweetened raspberries, thawed
    2   tablespoons plus 1 cup sugar
  2½   tablespoons imported crème de cassis (black-currant liqueur)

    6   large egg yolks
    2   cups whole milk
    2   cups heavy whipping cream
    1   tablespoon vanilla extract

For a berry swirl, add some sweetened crushed raspberries during the last minute of churning. The swirl may become icy after the ice cream is frozen, so soften slightly before serving.

Puree raspberries, 2 tablespoons sugar, and crème de cassis in processor. Let stand 15 minutes. Strain puree into bowl, pressing on seeds to extract as much fruit as possible; discard seeds.

Whisk yolks and 1 cup sugar in medium bowl to blend. Bring milk and cream to simmer in heavy medium saucepan. Gradually whisk hot cream mixture into yolk mixture; return custard to pan. Stir over medium heat until custard thickens enough to leave path on back of spoon when finger is drawn across, about 6 minutes (do not boil). Immediately pour custard into large bowl; mix in vanilla.

Place bowl of custard over another large bowl filled with ice and water and cool, stirring occasionally, about 40 minutes. Stir in raspberry puree.

Process custard in ice cream maker according to manufacturer's instructions. Transfer ice cream to large container, cover, and freeze until firm, at least 4 hours and up to 2 days.

MAKES ABOUT 6½ CUPS

Nectarine, Blackberry, and Pecan Sundaes

2   ½-pint containers blackberries
3   tablespoons (about) sugar

3   cups ½-inch cubes pitted nectarines (from about 5)
½   cup pecan pieces, toasted
1   to 2 pints vanilla ice cream

Puree blackberries in processor. Transfer puree to sieve set over bowl and strain, pressing with rubber spatula to extract as much pulp and juice as possible. Sweeten sauce to taste. *(Blackberry sauce can be made 1 day ahead. Cover and chill.)*

Place nectarines in medium bowl. Sweeten to taste, tossing with sugar 1 tablespoon at a time. Let stand 15 minutes. Spoon some sauce into bottom of 6 sundae dishes. Top with 2 tablespoons nectarines, some pecans, 2 scoops ice cream, more blackberry sauce, and more nectarines. Sprinkle with remaining pecans.

MAKES 6

Almond Florentine and Black Raspberry Chip Ice Cream Sandwiches

¼ cup (½ stick) unsalted butter

6 tablespoons sugar

¼ cup heavy whipping cream

2 tablespoons plus 1 teaspoon all purpose flour

¾ cup sliced almonds

1 pint black raspberry chip ice cream or other raspberry-flavored ice cream

Position rack in center of oven and preheat to 350°F. Line 2 large rimmed baking sheets with parchment paper. Melt butter in medium saucepan over medium-low heat. Mix in sugar, cream, and flour, then almonds. Stir until batter thickens, bubbles at edges, and leaves dry path when spoon is drawn through, about 10 minutes. Remove from heat. Drop 1 rounded teaspoonful batter for each cookie (about 24 total) onto prepared sheets, spacing mounds 2 to 3 inches apart.

Bake cookies, 1 sheet at a time, until golden brown, turning sheet after 8 minutes, about 16 minutes total. Cool cookies completely on sheets. (*Can be made 1 day ahead.* Store airtight at room temperature.)

Soften ice cream slightly in microwave at 10-second intervals on very low setting. Place 6 cookies, flat side up, on work surface. Mound ¼ cup ice cream onto each; flatten gently with spatula. Top with another cookie, flat side down, and press very gently to adhere. Place sandwiches on baking sheet, cover with foil, and freeze at least 2 hours and up to 2 days.

MAKES 6

Coffee-Almond Baked Alaska
with Coffee-Caramel Sauce

SAUCE

- 1 cup (packed) golden brown sugar
- ½ cup whipping cream
- ¼ cup (½ stick) unsalted butter
- 3 tablespoons brandy, divided
- 2 tablespoons dark corn syrup
- 1½ teaspoons instant espresso powder

CRUST AND ICE CREAM LAYERS

- 2 cups coarsely broken amaretti cookies* (about 4 ounces)
- 1 cup sliced almonds, toasted
- 2 teaspoons instant espresso powder
- 3 tablespoons unsalted butter, melted

- 3 pints almond hazelnut swirl or toasted almond ice cream
- 2 pints coffee ice cream

MERINGUE

- 6 large egg whites, room temperature
- ½ teaspoon vanilla extract
- 1 cup sugar

FOR SAUCE: Combine sugar, cream, butter, 2 tablespoons brandy, corn syrup, and espresso powder in medium saucepan. Whisk over medium heat until sugar dissolves. Increase heat to medium-high and boil until sauce is thickened and reduced to 1 cup, whisking often, about 8 minutes. Remove from heat; cool 15 minutes. Whisk in remaining 1 tablespoon brandy. Transfer to microwave-safe bowl.

FOR CRUST AND ICE CREAM LAYERS: Grind amaretti, almonds, and espresso powder in processor. Add butter and 1 tablespoon sauce. Blend just until crumbs cling together.

Line 10-inch-diameter, 3½-inch-high bowl (10-cup capacity) with plastic wrap, leaving long overhang. Slightly soften nut ice cream in microwave on defrost cycle for 10-second intervals. Spoon into bowl. Spread ice cream in even layer over bottom and up sides of bowl, leaving hollow center. Freeze 15 minutes. Press ⅔ cup crust mixture into ice cream. Slightly soften coffee ice cream in microwave on defrost setting for 10-second intervals. Spoon into center of ice cream mold; smooth top. Press remaining crust mixture over ice cream bombe. Cover with plastic. Freeze at least 3 hours. (*Can be made 2 days ahead. Keep frozen. Cover and chill remaining sauce.*)

FOR MERINGUE: Using electric mixer, beat egg whites and vanilla in large bowl until soft peaks form. Gradually add sugar, beating until meringue is stiff, about 5 minutes.

Uncover bombe. Place 11-inch-diameter tart pan bottom onto crust. Turn bombe over. Remove bowl; peel off plastic wrap. Spread meringue thickly over ice cream, swirling decoratively and sealing meringue to tart pan bottom. Place bombe uncovered in freezer at least 3 hours. *(Can be made 1 day ahead. Keep frozen.)*

Preheat oven to 500°F for 20 minutes. Rewarm sauce in microwave; transfer to pitcher. Place large rack on baking sheet. Place bombe on rack. Bake until meringue is pale golden but dark brown in spots, about 4 minutes; transfer to platter. Let stand 5 minutes.

Dipping heavy large knife into very hot water before each slice, cut bombe into wedges. Serve with sauce.

*Amaretti are light, airy Italian almond macaroons; available at some supermarkets and at Italian markets.

10 TO 12 SERVINGS

Two kinds of purchased ice cream get dressed up with a meringue topping and a rich sauce. A few minutes in a hot oven will give the meringue a golden glow.

Icy Lemon-Mint Parfaits

LEMON-MINT GRANITÉ

2 cups (loosely packed) fresh mint leaves plus 6 leaves for garnish

1¼ cups water

1 cup sugar

¾ cup fresh lemon juice

MINTED WHIPPED CREAM

¾ cup chilled heavy whipping cream

1½ tablespoons sugar

1½ tablespoons finely chopped fresh mint leaves

1 1-pint container fresh strawberries, hulled, thinly sliced

FOR LEMON-MINT GRANITÉ: Combine 2 cups mint leaves, 1¼ cups water, and sugar in medium saucepan. Stir over medium heat until sugar dissolves. Reduce heat to very low; cook 5 minutes without simmering. Pour syrup through fine strainer into 8x8x2-inch glass baking dish. Cool to room temperature; mix in lemon juice. Cover and freeze until firm, stirring occasionally, at least 6 hours or overnight.

FOR MINTED WHIPPED CREAM: Using electric mixer, beat cream, sugar, and mint in medium bowl until peaks form. *(Can be made 4 hours ahead. Cover and chill. Rewhisk to thicken before using.)*

Using fork, scrape granité to form crystals. Place 4 berry slices in each of 6 glasses. Top with 1 generous tablespoon minted cream, then 4 berry slices. Spoon ¼ cup granité over. Repeat layering with berry slices, minted cream, and granité. Garnish each parfait with berry slice and mint leaf.

6 SERVINGS

Key Lime Pie Sorbet

¾ cup water

½ cup sugar

1 14-ounce can sweetened condensed milk

1 cup fresh or bottled Key lime juice

Bring ¾ cup water and sugar to boil in heavy medium saucepan, stirring until sugar dissolves. Mix in sweetened condensed milk, then lime juice. Transfer mixture to medium bowl; place over large bowl filled with ice and water and cool, stirring often, about 30 minutes.

Process lime mixture in ice cream maker according to manufacturer's instructions. Transfer to medium container, cover, and freeze until firm, at least 4 hours and up to 2 days.

MAKES ABOUT 3 CUPS

Date and Walnut Phyllo Rolls with Greek Yogurt and Honey

14 ounces Medjool dates (about 1½ cups), pitted

½ cup walnuts, toasted

 3 tablespoons plus ¼ cup Greek honey or other honey

 1 teaspoon finely grated orange peel

½ teaspoon cardamom seeds (from about 10 pods), finely ground in spice mill or in mortar
    with pestle

 8 17½x12½-inch or sixteen 13½x8½-inch sheets fresh phyllo pastry or frozen, thawed

½ cup (1 stick) unsalted butter, melted

 1 cup Greek whole-milk yogurt

Combine dates, walnuts, 3 tablespoons honey, orange peel, and cardamom in processor. Blend until paste forms.

Preheat oven to 375°F. Line rimmed baking sheet with parchment. If using 17½ x 12½-inch phyllo sheets, place stack of 8 phyllo sheets on work surface. Halve stack crosswise, forming 16 sheets, each 12½ x 8¾ inches; arrange in 1 stack. Or if using 13½ x 8½-inch phyllo sheets, stack 16 sheets on work surface. Cover phyllo stack with plastic wrap, then damp kitchen towel. Remove 1 phyllo sheet from stack and place on work surface; brush with melted butter. Top with second sheet; brush with butter. Starting 1 inch from edge at short end of phyllo, spoon 3 tablespoons date mixture in dollops in row parallel to edge. Mold date mixture into log, leaving ½-inch border at edges of phyllo. Roll up date log in phyllo, enclosing filling and forming roll (filling will be exposed at ends). Transfer to baking sheet; brush with butter. Repeat with remaining phyllo, butter, and date mixture. Bake until golden, about 23 minutes. Cool on baking sheet.

Spoon yogurt into small bowl (or 8 individual bowls); drizzle remaining ¼ cup honey over yogurt. Place 1 phyllo roll on each of 8 plates. Serve with honeyed yogurt for dipping.

8 SERVINGS

Soft Ginger Cookies

- 4 cups all purpose flour
- 1 cup sugar
- 2 teaspoons baking soda
- 2 teaspoons ground ginger
- 1 teaspoon ground nutmeg
- 1 teaspoon ground cinnamon
- 1 teaspoon ground cloves
- ½ teaspoon salt
- 1 cup robust-flavored (dark) molasses
- ½ cup solid vegetable shortening
- 1 large egg, beaten to blend
- ½ cup boiling water

  Additional sugar

Combine first 8 ingredients in large bowl. Add molasses, shortening, and egg; beat to blend. Beat in boiling water. Chill 1 hour.

Preheat oven to 400°F. Roll chilled dough by tablespoonfuls into balls. Roll in additional sugar. Space balls 2 inches apart on ungreased baking sheets. Bake until cookies are puffed and cracked on top and centers still feel soft, about 12 minutes. Transfer to racks and cool.

MAKES ABOUT 40

Lunch on the Patio for 6

Mushroom-Shallot Quiche
(page 108)

Roasted Baby Beets and Arugula Salad with Lemon-Gorgonzola Vinaigrette
(page 141)

Iced Tea

Date and Walnut Phyllo Rolls with Greek Yogurt and Honey
(opposite; pictured opposite)

Chai-Spiced Almond Cookies

½ cup (1 stick) unsalted butter, room temperature
1⅓ cups powdered sugar, divided
2 teaspoons vanilla extract
1 teaspoon almond extract
¾ teaspoon ground allspice
¾ teaspoon ground cardamom
½ teaspoon ground cinnamon
¼ teaspoon salt
1 cup all purpose flour
¾ cup finely chopped toasted almonds

Preheat oven to 350°F. Using electric mixer, beat butter, ⅓ cup sugar, both extracts, spices, and salt in medium bowl. Beat in flour, then stir in almonds.

Using hands, roll dough into tablespoon-size balls. Place on large baking sheet, spacing apart. Bake until pale golden, about 25 minutes. Cool on sheet 5 minutes. Place remaining sugar in large bowl. Working in batches, gently coat hot cookies in sugar. Cool cookies on rack. Roll again in sugar and serve.

MAKES ABOUT 22

Milk Chocolate-Peanut Butter Sandwich Cookies

COOKIES

1¾ cups all purpose flour
1 teaspoon baking powder
½ teaspoon baking soda
½ teaspoon coarse kosher salt
½ cup plus ⅓ cup powdered sugar
½ cup plus 1 tablespoon (packed) dark brown sugar
6 tablespoons (¾ stick) unsalted butter, room temperature
½ cup creamy peanut butter
½ cup vegetable oil
1½ teaspoons vanilla extract
1 large egg
1⅓ cups (about 8 ounces) milk chocolate chips

FILLING

  3 ounces high-quality milk chocolate (such as Lindt or Perugina), chopped

¼ cup creamy peanut butter

  2 tablespoons powdered sugar

¼ teaspoon coarse kosher salt

  6 tablespoons whipping cream

FOR COOKIES: Preheat oven to 350°F. Whisk first 4 ingredients in medium bowl. Using electric mixer, beat powdered sugar, dark brown sugar, and butter in large bowl to blend. Add peanut butter; beat until creamy. Gradually beat in vegetable oil and vanilla extract, then egg. Add dry ingredients; mix just until blended. Stir in milk chocolate chips.

Drop cookie dough by level tablespoonfuls onto ungreased baking sheets, spacing about 1½ inches apart. Bake cookies until puffed and golden brown, about 12 minutes. Cool slightly, then transfer cookies to rack to cool completely.

FOR FILLING: Place chocolate, peanut butter, powdered sugar, and kosher salt in medium bowl. Bring whipping cream to boil in heavy small saucepan. Pour hot cream over chocolate mixture; stir until mixture is melted and smooth. Chill until filling is thick and spreadable, about 1 hour.

Spread about 1 rounded teaspoonful chocolate-peanut butter filling on flat side of 1 cookie. Top with second cookie, forming sandwich. Repeat with remaining filling and cookies. (*Cookie sandwiches can be made 1 day ahead. Store in airtight container at room temperature.*)

MAKES ABOUT 2½ DOZEN SANDWICH COOKIES

Be sure to use regular peanut butter—not old-fashioned or freshly ground—for the best consistency in the cookie batter and the filling.

Jamaican Coffee Brownies with Pecans

Nonstick vegetable oil spray
2 cups sugar
15 tablespoons (2 sticks minus 1 tablespoon) unsalted butter
¾ cup unsweetened cocoa powder
3 tablespoons finely ground Jamaican Blue Mountain coffee beans
½ teaspoon salt
3 large eggs
1½ teaspoons vanilla extract
1¼ cups all purpose flour
¾ cup pecan pieces

1 cup bittersweet or semisweet chocolate chips (6 ounces)
6 tablespoons freshly brewed Jamaican Blue Mountain coffee

30 thin strips crystallized ginger (optional)

Preheat oven to 350°F. Spray 13x9x2-inch metal pan with nonstick spray. Combine sugar, butter, cocoa, ground coffee, and salt in large metal bowl. Place bowl over saucepan of simmering water and whisk until butter melts and ingredients are blended (texture will be grainy). Remove bowl from over water; cool mixture to lukewarm if necessary. Whisk in eggs and vanilla. Sift flour over and fold in. Mix in pecans.

Spread batter in prepared pan. Bake brownies until tester inserted into center comes out clean, about 25 minutes. Cool brownies in pan.

Place chocolate chips in small bowl. Bring brewed coffee to simmer in small saucepan; pour over chips and stir until melted and smooth. Let ganache stand until cool and beginning to thicken, about 1 hour; spread evenly over brownies. (*Can be made 1 day ahead. Cover; let stand at room temperature.*)

Cut brownies into 15 squares. Top each with 2 ginger strips, if desired.

MAKES 15

Almond Macaroons

1½ cups whole almonds (7 to 8 ounces)
¾ cup sugar
1½ large egg whites (about 3 tablespoons)
¾ teaspoon vanilla extract

Preheat oven to 400°F. Line large baking sheet with parchment paper. Blend almonds and sugar in processor until nuts are finely ground. Add egg whites and vanilla. Blend, using on/off turns, until batter is thick and sticky. Using wet hands, shape batter by tablespoonfuls into balls. Arrange on baking sheet, spacing about 1½ inches apart (cookies will spread slightly); brush with water.

Bake macaroons until golden, about 18 minutes. Slide parchment onto large rack. Cool macaroons completely on parchment. Run knife under macaroons to loosen. Store airtight up to 2 days.

MAKES ABOUT 22

Black and White Chocolate Chunk Cookies

Nonstick vegetable oil spray
2 cups all purpose flour
¾ cup unsweetened cocoa powder
1 teaspoon baking soda
¾ teaspoon salt
¾ cup sugar
¾ cup (packed) golden brown sugar
½ cup solid vegetable shortening
½ cup (1 stick) unsalted butter, room temperature
2 large eggs
1 teaspoon vanilla extract
12 ounces coarsely chopped high-quality white chocolate (such as Lindt or Perugina)
1 cup coarsely chopped pecans

Preheat oven to 350°F. Spray 2 baking sheets with nonstick spray. Whisk flour, cocoa powder, baking soda, and salt in medium bowl. Using electric mixer, beat both sugars, shortening, and butter in large bowl until fluffy. Beat in eggs and vanilla. Add dry ingredients; stir. Add white chocolate and pecans; stir.

Drop dough by tablespoonfuls onto prepared baking sheets, spacing 2 inches apart; flatten slightly. Bake cookies until just set, about 13 minutes. Cool on racks. (*Can be made 3 days ahead.*) Store airtight at room temperature.

MAKES ABOUT 3 DOZEN

Pumpkin Cheesecake Crumble Squares

CRUST

- 1 cup all purpose flour
- ¾ cup (packed) golden brown sugar
- ½ teaspoon salt
- ½ cup (1 stick) chilled unsalted butter, diced
- 1 cup pecan halves (about 4 ounces)
- ¾ cup old-fashioned oats

FILLING

- 1 8-ounce package cream cheese, room temperature
- ¾ cup canned pure pumpkin
- ½ cup sugar
- 1 large egg
- 1½ teaspoons ground cinnamon
- 1 teaspoon ground ginger

TOPPING

- 1 cup sour cream
- 2 tablespoons sugar
- ¼ teaspoon vanilla extract

FOR CRUST: Preheat oven to 350°F. Generously butter 9x9x2-inch metal baking pan. Line rimmed baking sheet with parchment. Using on/off turns, blend first 4 ingredients in processor until coarse meal forms. Add pecans; using on/off turns, process until nuts are chopped. Add oats; process using on/off turns until mixture is moistened but not clumping. Press 3½ cups crumbs onto bottom of prepared square pan (do not clean processor). Transfer remaining crumbs to lined baking sheet. Bake crumbs on sheet until golden, stirring once, about 12 minutes. Cool crumbs. Bake crust until golden, about 30 minutes. Remove from oven while preparing filling. Maintain oven temperature.

FOR FILLING: Blend all ingredients in same processor until smooth. Spread filling over warm crust; bake until set, dry in center, and beginning to rise at edges, about 20 minutes. Maintain oven temperature.

FOR TOPPING: Mix all ingredients in small bowl. Spread evenly over hot filling. Bake until topping sets and bubbles at edges, about 5 minutes. Cool completely in pan on rack. Sprinkle crumbs over topping; gently press into topping. Cover; chill until cold, about 2 hours. (*Can be made 2 days ahead. Keep chilled.*) Cut into squares.

MAKES 16

Index

Page numbers in *italics* indicate color photographs.

Acknowledgments

RECIPES
Bruce Aidells
Bartolotta Ristorante di Mare,
    Las Vegas, Nevada
Lena Cederham Birnbaum
Blue Heron Restaurant,
    Sunderland, Massachusetts
Julia Boorstin
Rick Browne
Ken Callaghan
Mary Cech
Cat Cora
Paula and Taras Danyluk
Giada De Laurentiis
Karen DeMasco
David Downie
Susan Elizabeth Fallon
Elizabeth Falkner
Charlotte Fekete
Barbara Pool Fenzl
Anne Marie Gaspard
Ann Gillespie
Miriyam Glazer
Phyllis Glazer
Todd Goddard
Suzanne Goin

Hedy Goldsmith
Karin and Ian Goodfellow
Dorie Greenspan
Brian S. Hale
George Hendrix
Katy Hees
Cara Brunetti Hillyard
Susanna Hoffman
Jill Silverman Hough
Kingsley John
Elizabeth Karmel
Jeanne Thiel Kelley
Melissa Kelly
Kristine Kidd
Paul Kirk
Kitchen 1924, Dallas, Texas
Michael Kohn
Stacy Kuiack
Donald Link
Beatriz Llamas
Michael Lomonaco
Emily Luchetti
Janet Taylor McCracken
Andrew Mandolene
Sal Marino
Daisy Martinez

Tina Miller
Brenda and Scott Mitchell
Diana Morrison
Selma Brown Morrow
Florence Myers
Brandi Neuwirth
Nancy Oakes
Alfred Portale
Anna Pump
Victoria Abbott Riccardi
Eric Ripert
Tori Ritchie
Rick Rodgers
Douglas Rodriguez
Maury Rubin
Audrey Saunders
Michael Schlow
Schooner Isaac H. Evans
Barbara Scott-Goodman
Norma Shirley
Maria Helm Sinskey
Katy Sparks
Molly Stevens
Caroline Styne
Allen Susser
Table 8, Los Angeles, California

Sarah Tenaglia
Suzanne Tracht
Rori Trovato
Carolyn Beth Weil
Diane Rossen Worthington

PHOTOGRAPHY
Sang An
Noel Barnhurst
Maren Caruso
Gemma Comas
Wyatt Counts
Daniel Hennessy
Lisa Hubbard
Ray Kachatorian
Kevin Keith
Brian Leatart
Pornchai Mittongtare
Gary Moss
Ngoc Minh Ngo
Victoria Pearson
Scott Peterson
Tina Rupp
Mark Thomas
Luca Trovato